AFRO-MAN
AND THE PROTECTORS OF THE BOOK OF KNOWLEDGE

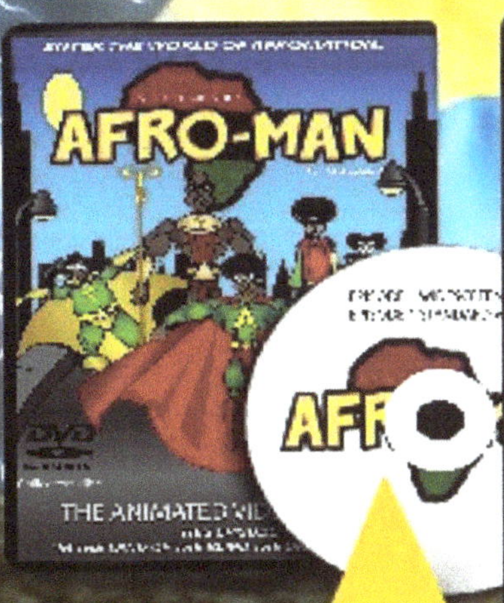

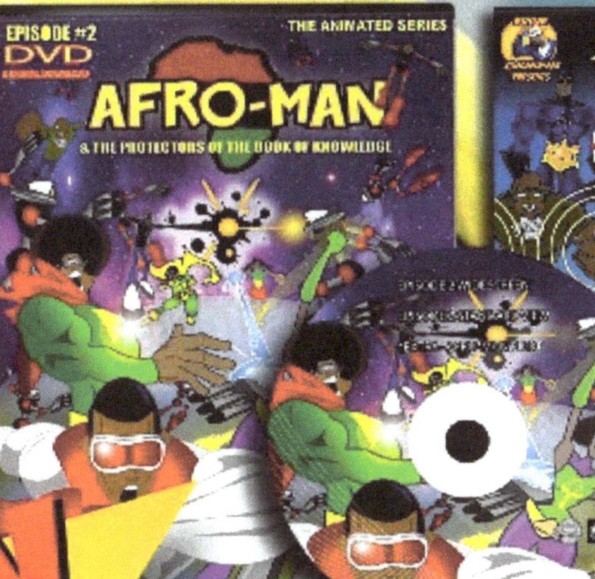

BUY NOW!

THE ANIMATED SERIES

WWW.AFROMANKIDSSPACE.COM

CONTENTS

Tachyon Node Volume 1 Issue 3

January 2016

ISSN 2379-982X

Mythical Legends Publishing
First printed 2015
P.O. Box 1667
Inglewood, Ca. 90308

J Carrell Jones, Publisher and Editor-in-Chief
Editorial Staff
Patricia I Williams, Reader

Contributing Writers
Moshe Prigan
Jarita Holbrook, Ph.D
Tonya moore
Patricia I Williams
Devon Nicholson
Brandon Hill
Kenneth A. Strickland
J Carrell Jones

Cover Art by Cesar Valtierra
Black Hole image, pg. 37, NASA/JPL-Caltech
http://www.nasa.gov/nustar

Contributing Artist to Rogue's Gallery
Björn Malmberg
Ryan
J Carrell Jones

Article/Story Submissions:
Publisher@mythicallegends.com
Advertisement:
Ads@mythicallegends.com
General Information:
Info@mythicallegends.com or send snail mail to
Mythical Legends Publishing
c/o General Information
P.O. Box 1667
Inglewood, Ca. 90308

ISSN 2379-982X
ISBN-13: 978-1-943958-51-1

Printed in the United States of America

Dimensional Nexus

Staff Thoughts

Rogue's Gallery

Data Node

Bibliography

Moshe Prigan
Tonya Moore
Devon Nicholson
Kenneth A. Strickland
Jarita Holbrook, Ph.D
Patricia I Williams
Brandon Hill
J Carrell Jones

FOLKTALES
COMIC REPUBLIC
3
ĒRU
FEAR ITSELF
ĒRU
OUT NOW
EZEOGU
EZEOGU
IKECHUKWU
WWW.THECOMICREPUBLIC.COM

GEMP

by J Carrell Jones **Final Part**

Chapter 8

Steve, Kelly, and Oscar were still in the lunch room when Grenier approached their table.

Kelly gestured for him to join.

Oscar jumped from his seat.

Grenier caught him and gave Oscar a head bump.

The chimp grinned teeth and cooed.

Grenier sat down placing Oscar next to him. "I got good news and bad news."

Steve nodded, "We heard the announcement over the PA."

Grenier smiled, "That's part of the good news."

Kelly asked, "What's the bad news?" She had her hand on Steve's arm.

His smile faded, "Because of our friend the Colonel, the project is being shut down."

"That's terrible news!" Steve said.

Kelly asked, "What's going to happen to the Gemps?"

Grenier's smile returned. "We're moving to phase 2 of the project. We are . . ."

Steve said, "Wait. Phase 2?"

Grenier nodded. "You didn't think Uncle Sam would use the Gemps for religious studies their entire lives?"

Steve slowly shook his head.

"At some point we'd have to deal with superstitious Gemps. Now is probably better than later."

Steve took a deep breath, "Okay, what is phase 2?"

Grenier stood up. "Follow me to my office and we can talk."

***

Pierce and a dozen soldiers stood in the Colonel's room.

Codper had put the bottle down and now faced them. He shaved and had his ACU on. The bible was in his left hand. "Those creatures out there are a threat to the natural order of things. In our arrogance we created life in His image, but life as an abomination. An un-pure monstrosity

that mocks our very existence. This mockery ends today."

The men around him nodded.

Pierce stepped out. "Colonel, of course, we're with you. They have to go. Everything has to go."

Codper asked, "I take it you've worked out details?"

Pierce rapidly sucked in air between his front teeth. The smack sound was loud. "Of course, sir. And with your approval."

Codper studied the young man. Was he one to trust? Probably not, but how was he supposed to save his kind. "Let's hear it."

"First, we gather everyone into one room. Then we capture some wild Gemps and toss them in the room with the others. We shoot a few folks and Gemps and toss in some grenades. Then we release the other Gemps and hunt them down under the pretense they are dangerous. Once that's done, we call in for help. Blame everything on the Gemps and a few soldiers not with us. While we were out getting the village Gemps, the "other" soldiers got too sloppy. We can guess the wild Gemps either got the grenades by accident and not knowing what to do killed themselves and everyone in the room or some fool soldier held on too long. We stick to our story that we tried to round up the village Gemps and the deed is done."

Codper nodded. He liked the plan. Factor in the fog of war and Pierce had a pretty good plan. "And we are the survivors."

Pierce nodded. "We give each man in this room a story to tell. Not the same story of course, different enough. Someone was by the door. Another person was down the hall. Someone saw some Gemps in the building. Some did not but heard Gemp screams."

Codper nodded.

"We'll also have to beat ourselves up a bit to make it convincing we fought for our lives. But we can pull this off."

Codper slowly smiled. "We could pull this off. I like it."

"Thank you, sir." He turned to face one of those is the room. "Donalds. Turn off the video and audio feeds. Internal and external. McKinney, you, Rich,

and Smithie release the wild Gemps. Capture a few and cuff'em. Ford, Luke, Rogers, Threatt, secure the control room. The rest is with me and the Colonel. We'll round up Launse, Grenier and the others. I got more of us guarding the exits just waiting for the word."

Codper thought a moment, then quickly nodded. "Let's do this."

***

Grenier walked in first and sat behind his desk. Steve and Kelly took a seat with Oscar jumping into Steve's lap.

"Would anyone care for coffee?" Grenier asked.

Oscar signed, "Coffee, please."

Grenier smiled. "Certainly, Oscar. The usual amount of sugar and cream?"

Oscar signed, "Yes, please. Sugar, yum."

Grenier got up and walked over to a small kitchenette at the corner of his office. "First, phase 2 is about teaching the Gemps basic common core lessons." He put in two scoops of instant coffee grounds into a coffee mug. Oscar's name was stenciled across the side. "The government wants the Gemps taught at a college level and . . ."

Steve interrupted, ". . . taught! As in attending school?"

Grenier scooped in two heaping piles of sugar using a small spoon. He poured about two seconds worth of cream. He stirred the spoon as he poured hot water into the cup. After a moment of stirring he walked over to Oscar and handed the cup of coffee to him.

Oscar took the cup and sipped. Just the way he liked it.

Steve cleared his throat, "As in attending school?"

Grenier nodded slowly, "Something like that."

Kelly leaned forward, "Ken, what are you not telling us?"

No need to withhold any information now, Grenier thought. "Space is a pretty dangerous place . . ." He continued before Steve or Kelly interrupted, ". . . so is underwater exploration. So is sub-terrain discovery expeditions.   Sending Soldiers behind enemy lines is also dangerous work." He paused for several seconds. "You see where I'm going with this?"

Steve horrified, answered, "I do and I don't know how I'm feeling about that."

Grenier turned to Kelly. "What are your thoughts?"

Kelly looked at Steve and Oscar, then back at him. "It'll initially save their lives?"

Grenier thought she had been the quicker of the two. Steve was much too nostalgic and emotional. Kelly he liked a bit more than he often admitted. She was more pragmatic.

"What about their rights?" Kelly asked.

"As of now, they have none. They are all property of the United States Government, but to put your mind at ease, they will not be overlooked per se."

Steve interjected, "Per se?"

"The Gemps are highly intelligent creatures. They have emotions. They think and more importantly, they can learn, of which is what makes them valuable."

"They shouldn't be thought of as property." Steve said.

Grenier shrugged and held it for a few seconds. He pursed his lips and raised both eyebrows. "I don't have an answer for that. Not a good one. But I can tell you, that one day the Gemps will be granted full US Citizen status. But not today. Maybe not in a few years."

Steve asked, "How come?"

"We had a hard time dealing with a debt ceiling. We have ultra conservatives in our government who'll toss out the baby with the bathwater. We've been working quietly to get this far. The Gemps are under a provision that guarantees humane treatment and plans for their free retirement."

Steve shook his head. "So much I'm not quite getting."

Oscar kissed him on the cheek.

Grenier continued, "The Gemps will be allowed certain privileges . . ."

Kelly asked, ". . . like?"

"Clothes, foods, certain types of property, some things we have to educate the population first before they can walk freely. We're working out the details of pay . . ."

Steve frowned. "Pay?"

"Yeah. Even if the Gemps aren't citizens they will still work. We can't call them beast of burden. They aren't farm animals. The one advantage they have, unlike the dolphins or Oscar, is that they can articulate emotions, desires, wants, and needs. Can you imagine the lawsuits from every Lib-organization on Earth if we didn't treat them like people?"

Steve's frown deepened.

"Steve, this nation still can't quite get it right with minorities. How do you think the neo-conservative is going to react to genetically-engineered super-intelligent teenage-like chimps walking freely? We'll have another sort of problems with the active left as well."

Steve started, "But . . ."

Grenier said, ". . . no buts. Warm and fuzzy this can't be yet."

Steve took a deep breath. "Okay, what is our role?"

Grenier relaxed a bit. "Mentor and instructor. I'll be getting involved in this phase."

"As what?" Steve asked.

Oscar finished his coffee and stretched out on Steve's lap. Coffee made him feel good but sleepy sometimes. Or it could have been that he was only able to understand and follow a small part of what Grenier talked about. Humans talked too much sometimes. They made him sleepy.

"Depends on the task."

Kelly added, "Mission?"

Grenier nodded. "Yeah, the mission. I just don't push paper."

Suddenly the alarm went off.

Grenier punched in the speed dial code to the Main Command center. It rang a dozen times before he got a disconnect tone. "Fuck! This is not good." He walked over to the door and opened it. Just as he suspected. "Greetings Colonel, Captain Pierce, I was just . . ."

Codper punched him in the face a second time today.

Grenier stepped back a few feet and rubbed his jaw. "That hurt."

Codper drew his pistol and pointed it directly at his face. "You pompous ass. Give me a reason not to shoot you in the face now." He stepped up close to Grenier. Pierce and the rest had M16-A2s pointed at him.

Grenier grabbed the gun and pressed it hard against Codper's thigh dislocating the trigger finger at the knuckle.

Codper bit down a yell.

Grenier pulled the gun away and pointed it at Codper's face. "You pompous arrogant ass back. Any other time I would have shot you in the face and not given you a second thought. I know how this is going to play out." He pressed the magazine release and caught it with his left hand. Bullets flipped toward Codper's face as he emptied the clip. He tossed the magazine across the room and dismantled the Beretta M9. He chucked the barrel behind his desk and spun the handle at Codper.

Codper was nursing his dislocated finger when the handle clipped him across the forehead. It left a nasty gash. The Colonel took a deep breath and popped his finger back in place. He walked over and gave Grenier a slap with the other hand. "You . . . you . . ."

Grenier walked out into the hallway. Other soldiers stood attentive with pointed M16s.

Oscar signed, "Me bite Colonel?"

Steve signed back, "No bite Colonel. Bite will make you sick."

Codper faced Steve and Kelly. "Launse, Ma'am, please follow Grenier."

Oscar growled.

Steve grabbed Oscar's face, "No growl. Be good." He and Kelly walked into the hall way and followed Grenier and the other soldiers.

Codper said, "Nasty beast. If I had my gun I'd shoot the thing."

Pierce watched everything. He liked Oscar. Pretty much everyone did. Strike three for the Colonel.

***

Grenier heard several explosives. His first impulse was to run toward the sound. The M16s at his back squelched it. A second impulse wanted him to take Steve and the others in the opposite direction. The smell of death was in the air and he saw no happy ending to this day.

Codper moved ahead and hurried down the stairs. The doors to one of the rooms had been blown out. Scorched body parts and debris littered the entrance. "What the fuck happened?"

A nearby soldier said, "Someone tried to be a hero, sir. Boom."

Codper turned to face Pierce.

Pierce shrugged. "There's more than one room. You want to shoot them in the back?"

Codper answered, "I wanted this to be clean and quick. Now it's . . ."

Grenier never let him finish. He grabbed the nearest M16, switched the selector to single shoot and squeezed the trigger once at the soldier's face. Blood splattered in all direction. He squeezed off several more shots – all hitting dead center. "Run!" He yelled.

Steve and Kelly ducked behind a station desk. Bullets sprayed the area in fits and blurps across the room.

Grenier squeezed off several single shots in seemingly random directions – all finding a target.

Then, the shooting stopped.

Grenier looked up and saw several Grenades tossed his way. Five second fuses he thought as he jumped over the desk and caught two mid-flight. He twisted and threw both at the emergency door across the room. He landed near Steve, Kelly, and Oscar. One second to go he thought as he dragged the desk just enough to shelter everyone from the blasts.

Oscar screamed as the first grenade blew. He squeezed Steve's neck tightly. The blast pushed them and the desk several feet. Two more explosions went off further away.

Grenier's ears rang. He shook his head to clear the fog.

Steve, Kelly, and Oscar seemed alright. Steve looked as if he were about to pass out. Oscar had a death grip, with long chimp arms, around his neck.

Grenier grabbed everyone and made them run

to the new hole in the wall. The emergency doors gone.

Codper waited several seconds after the grenades went off. He stepped in the room and expected to see body parts and blood splatter everywhere. "What the fuck!" Only desk and computer debris scattered the room. He looked around and saw the emergency doors missing. Things got complicated.

***

Tutu sat against a large rock near the remains of an old fire. Burnt logs buried in ashes jetted out. Tonight they would start another fire and roast corn from the mystery box. He finished one apple and started eating a second one when he smelled dirty fur. He wrinkled his nose and turned to the forest edge. Immediately, the hair at the back of his neck stiffened. Intruder.

"Food," the figure said.

Tutu strained to see the figure just inside the tree line. It hugged close to the ground.

"Food. Food want."

Tutu took several steps back adding some distance between him and the strange creature. "Show self. Then food get."

The figure retreated further into the forest

Tutu took a step forward, stopped, thought a moment, took several more steps back. "Want food. Show self."

The figure moved. It was quick.

Tutu tried to track it visually as it faded further into the forest. Moments later the figure was gone and he heard a scream. He turned and ran. It was from one of the female village Gemps.

Strange looking Gemps had invaded his village. Within seconds the village was overrun by filthy intruders. A wild Gemp jumped him. He twisted underneath it and swung his arm backward. He felt his fist contact teeth and something gave way. The wild Gemp lay motionless on the ground. A wild Gemp was on Mos trying to bite his neck. Tutu clenched his hands together and gave it a powerful downward blow to the head. The wild Gemp's skull caved in and the creature went limp.

Mos looked up and gave Tutu a "thank you" sign.

Both Gemps looked on and attacked as many wild Gemps as possible. Two jumped on Mos. Three on Tutu.

Oscar ran ahead of the others. He heard the commotion and feared the worst. Hela and Feme in trouble. Hurry he thought. Hurry. Hela Feme in trouble. Must help. Run faster. On some subsurface level Oscar knew things had suddenly changed. The Colonel, Pierce, most of the men on the base. They were different. The explosions. The pieces of people and the shooting. All scary. All terrifying.

Lulos was on the ground. She struggled as a wild Gemp tried to mount her. She screamed, kicked, and screamed more.

The wild Gemp became rock solid. This he was going to enjoy. He grabbed Lulos' neck and started to squeeze. Just as he was about to enter Oscar jumped him. Powerful chimp arms pounded hard about his head and shoulders. The wild Gemp tried to get away, but Oscar's attack was relentless. Moments later the wild Gemp stopped fighting back.

Steve, Kelly, and Grenier arrived to see Oscar step off the dead Gemp. They heard several screams toward the center of the village.

Oscar moved first. These were his Gemps. No creature he thought would harm them. Ever. The wild Gemps were attacking the others. Grenier ran over to two wild Gemps attacking Mos. Both were biting at and hitting him. Grenier grabbed one Gemp and placed a choke hold on it. It screamed and clawed at his face. Seconds later it went limp. A second later Grenier broke its neck. He hated to, Uncle Sam's money or not, this was survival now.

Mos swung upward and hit the other Gemp in the jaw. It broke but the thing continued attacking. Mos swung again as hard as he could. His arms ached. He swung again and again. He hit the face. He hit the head. He hit the head again. And again. And again. He stood over a dead Gemp.

Steve stood motionless watching pandemonium. He saw Grenier and Oscar in action, helping as they could. Even Kelly tried to help. She kicked at a wild Gemp trying to rape a female. She pulled its hair and punched its face. Soon, both females were beating the poor creature into unconsciousness. Then a wild Gemp jumped on Kelly. It bite her in the shoulder and she screamed. He acted. He screamed like Oscar and struck at the animal. His anger was primal and fierce. His attack was ruthless. The wild Gemp cringed as Steve pounded with all his might. Kelly was his love and no man or creature would harm her. He continued pounding at its chest and skull until it lay still. He breathed hard, his heart pounding. Murder is what he just committed. With his hands. He turned on the other wild Gemps. A dozen left. Attacking. He leapt into action alongside Oscar and fought. Both of them crazed creatures raining powerful blows down on the invaders.

Mos looked on in awe. God and the Elder defending the village. The screams the two made. High pitched and terrifying. Mos looked at both his hands and made fists. He joined the fray, not quite getting the yell right. But after a moment he too was caught up in the frenzy. Arms high, power down, scream loud. Make the wild ones fear their wrath. The wrath of God, Elder . . . and the Messenger.

Then . . . silence.

The village littered with dead and wounded wild Gemps.

Steve was bruised badly across the cheek and arm. His clothing torn.

Kelly's face was covered with dirt, her makeup smudged.

Oscar's robe colored with dirt and blood.

Grenier looked perfect. His suit wrinkle free and his hair neatly combed.

Mos walked up to Steve, "God, you saved us."

Tutu walked up to Steve. He looked at Grenier and Kelly, then turned his gaze back to Steve. "Something not right. There is more than one of you. And these other Gemps?"

Grenier and Kelly walked up next to Steve. He faced Tutu. "You are right." He looked at Mos. "We

have to talk. Things are about to change. And I have to be honest with you."

Mos said, "Honest? With me?

Steve nodded. He looked at Tutu. "Others like us may be coming. The others are bad. They are the reason these other Gemps are here."

Tutu growled. "Hate other Gemps. Crazy." He then looked at Steve, Kelly, and Grenier. Clothing strange, faces strange, all things strange. "What does God mean?"

Steve answered, "You have to send the village Gemps in the forest. To hide. I fear the worst."

Tutu repeated, "What does God mean?"

Grenier leaned close to Steve. "I think he wants to know the meaning of God. Not what you are saying as God."

Steve looked at Grenier for a moment, then he looked at Tutu. Those eyes Steve thought. Tutu is the one, not Mos. "Tutu, I am not God."

Mos, distressed, said, "God must not say such things. Mos see great scary things from God."

Steve knelt down. "I wish we had time to explain, but we really must hide. Everyone."

Grenier said, "I called in a support team earlier. Don't know how long they will take so, in the meantime, keeping out of sight is best."

Tutu said, "We will stay. No run."

Steve frowned. "Tutu, we are not running. We are hiding. We . . ."

". . . no, I am not God. We . . ."

". . . must hide." Steve stressed.

Tutu shook his head slowly. "No."

Steve looked to Grenier.

Grenier said, "We're probably priority one. The Gemps are secondary. "

Oscar suddenly looked alert. He pried into the forest toward the main building. He growled.

Grenier said, "Yeah, I don't like them either. We should leave now. Staying in the village is definitely not in the Gemps best interest."

Oscar yelped and jumped into Steve's arm.

Grenier lead the way. He and the others disappeared in the forest.

Moments later Tutu heard a rumbling sound.

Mos stepped up next to him. He strained his eyes. "I hear sound too. Things are different now."

Tutu nodded.

The rest of the village Gemps started to assemble near Tutu and Mos.

Kiri stood next to Mos.

Hela and Feme were near.

The sound got louder and the ground vibrated.

Tutu caught a whiff of exhaust. He wrinkled his noise and growled.

A moment later a Humvee crashed through the tree line, followed by several more. Most of the Gemps scattered. Mos thought they looked like wide hollowed out tree trunks. Men like 'I am not God' came through wearing strange colored clothing. They had thick sticks and strange tree branches in their arms. One of the strangers held a small "L" shaped stick. He pointed it at one of the Gemps. Thunder and smoked ripped from a hole at one end.

Mos watched as blood spattered from the Gemp's head. It crumpled to the ground. Fear gripped Mos. God had been right. "Run!" He yelled out, "Run!" Tutu ran with him as rapid thunder erupted from the thick sticks and branches the evil creatures held. "Run!" Kiri, Hela and Feme were near and followed as Mos crashed through the jungle. The last time he ran he met God. This time it was because of God again.

Codper saw the vile creatures scatter into the jungle. He put a bullet in one of them and it felt satisfying. "Kill them all!" He shouted. "Kill them all!"

Chapter 9

Captain Pierce looked on as his men and the Colonel hunted the Gemps down. He thought they would have made great pets – especially the females. He watched the bootlegged copies of more than one Gemp sex video. Some of the soldiers, he thought, were sick perverts. They talked about how big the Males got and called them Nickers. When he finally caved in and watched his first video he came within minutes. His guilty thoughts on how young the females looked made him sick to his stomach. It took five more viewings before guilt disappeared entirely. Now he was shooting them. He gave a heavy sign as one female came into view. She was running toward him not looking. He lifted up his rifle and laid the crosshair square center of her chest. She had small breasts that jiggled tightly as she bound over rocks and fallen tree branches. He pulled his finger away from the trigger and quickly scanned the area near her. She was alone. Pierce's palms started to sweat. He moved the scope back on the Gemp. She was still running toward him. He shouldered his rifle and slid behind a tree, waiting. His strike would be swift.

Wela ran as fast as she could. The bad creatures had been hurting the others and she had to find safe shelter.

Pierce waited and heard the Gemp rapidly move his way. When he saw an outstretched furry arm he grabbed it.

Wela was too shocked to say anything. The bad creature's grip was powerful. He pulled her in close to his chest and put a hand around her mouth. She found his thumb just above her lip. His other hand started groping her chests. She tried to scream but his hand gripped tighter around her mouth. She grabbed his wrist and pulled down. His thumb touched her lips and she clamped on to it with her teeth. He hit her in the back of the head. She bite down hard between the distal joint. Skin gave way and her teeth cut neatly through muscle, tendon, and cartilage. He pushed her away screaming at her. She backed off and spat the thumb out of her mouth. He aimed the rifle and squeezed off a round. The bullet missed her heart but pierced her left shoulder slicing through the lung and shattering the top part of shoulder blade. She fainted.

Pierce cursed himself and spat at the Gemp. He stepped up to Wela and rolled her over. He ripped her loin-cloth off making her cheeks quiver. He stared at her butt and fantasized abusing it until the arch in his thumb became unbearable. He wrapped the cloth tightly around his wound and considered his options. "Stupid little bitch." He uttered. "I ought to fucking rape your chimp ass." He stared intently at Wela licking his lips. He sucked in air between his front teeth and lips. The pain in his thumb faded. He knelt down on top of Wela and started rubbing himself on her. He could feel himself aroused and he rubbed harder. He pulled himself out and started stroking with his right hand. "You vile little bitch. I'm gonna make you suck." He rolled the unconscious Wela on to her back and moved himself up to her mouth. He played himself across her lips getting himself wet. When he was about to explode he slipped himself into Wela's mouth and pumped fervently. Seconds later he erupted. His entire body spasmed like never before. It was intense and extreme.

Wela woke up with a start. The bad creature had himself in her mouth and she nearly gagged when he jismed. She was not afraid this time, but angry. No male Gemp would do such a thing unless given permission. She looked up and saw the bad creature, with closed eyes, shaking. She scowled and bit down as if she were biting into a rock. Stiffened tissue split and her upper and bottom teeth met hard. The man screamed loudly as blood pumped out from what was left of his penis. Wela had bitten off more than half. The bad creature fumbled for his rifle. Wela coughed strongly causing her to gag and vomit the soft piece out. She hissed at Pierce, wiped her mouth and disappeared into the forest.

Pierce fired his rifle at the receding Wela. His aim was off due to throbbing pain from two embarrassing wounds, which could never be adequately explained.

***

Grenier made it to a crop of rocks at the bottom of the mountain. Kelly and Steve, breathing hard, emerged from the jungle tree line and collapsed at Grenier's feet. Oscar had been sitting on a ledge, waiting, for some minutes. He knew the area well.

Grenier said, "Okay, we make a stand here . . ."

Steve, still breathing hard, said, ". . . what stand? They have guns we have nothing."

Grenier shook his head, "Wrong thinking. We have everything we need. We have Oscar, you, Kelly,

myself. We have rocks and the high ground . . ."

Steve said, ". . . we can't fight guns with rocks!"

"We have to hold them off until the cavalry arrives. Might be hours, might be days. But we have to try. Hiding is not an option. Not with me."

Steve answered, "Fuck!"

Grenier squared-off in front of the younger man, "Steve, trust me on this. We have the advantage."

"I want too, but . . ."

"Steve, why this spot? I ran you guys three miles through dense jungle to here. Oscar knows this place, you should too."

Steve, breathe caught, looked around. He spotted a remote camera high in one of the trees. Near the base on the mountain he spotted a strange pattern of rocks. They were stacked rather neatly. The bottom rock had a small black ring near its bottom. The top rock had a small metal nipple in front.

Grenier interrupted his thoughts, "You remember now?"

Steve smiled. Hope was not lost.

Tutu caught the Elder's scent quickly. I am not God's scent was faint but distinct. He wanted answers. The village was attacked by dirty smelling Gemps and bad creatures. He quickened his pace.

Mos followed Tutu through the underbrush. This area on The Place was thick with trees and plants. Further out was the salty water and the sand. There were lots of scary caves that held strange lights and sounds. Mos had forgotten about the caves. He remembered an encounter some time ago and started to slow down.

Kiri came up beside him, "Mos, you slow down?"

Mos picked up his pace. "Mos okay."

Kiri wondered.

Grenier entered the access code to the observation room. It was situated deep in one of the many caves that dotted the mountain side. The last time they used it was about two years ago, but it was still functional and had a cache of food, clothing, weapons, and communication equipment.

Tutu followed the scents to a cave entrance some

ten feet above the ground. He remembered this one in particular. Strange noises and lights came from deep inside it. At the time he was afraid to further investigate. He was young and scared easily back then.

Mos remembered this cave as well. Tutu told him of the lights and noise. He was curious and made the long trip to see for himself. Smoke was coming from one of the rocks and he heard moans. The fur on the back of his neck stiffened and he couldn't go any further. Now he stood in front on the very cave that scared him not so long ago.

Kiri, Hela, and Feme stood next to the two male Gemps. They noticed the expressions on each of their faces. Tutu was purposeful. Mos was dread.

Grenier had just settled into a command station. He flipped the power switch to the chamber earlier and waited a minute for all the computers and systems to come online. A proximity alert went off. "Fuck! Not now!" He typed in a code and the remote cameras searched the area. Tutu, Mos, and several other Gemps were at the base of the cave. He smiled and exhaled. Maybe this was the best time to wean the Gemps off mother's milk. "Steve," he said, "we have company."

Steve stepped over to the Monitor. "We have to get them in here."

Grenier nodded, but for different reasons. "I'm changing the access codes to all the doors . . . belay that. I'm leaving the exterior door alone. We'll have to pull out some food before the Colonel and friends finds us."

Tutu and Mos helped the other Gemps scale the ten foot climb to the cave entrance. Mos caught the Elder's scent. He wasn't sure if he should be glad or upset.

Tutu stepped into the cave first.

Mos hesitated a moment.

Kiri placed a hand on his shoulder, "Mos . . ."

Mos nearly jumped. He gave Kiri a glance and he followed Tutu into the cave.

Steve stepped out into the tunnel and stayed within the shadows. He watched the Gemps inch their way along the cave wall until Tutu was about five feet in front of him. "Stop." He said.

Tutu, startled, hissed. He squinted his eyes and a faint image of Steve appeared. "What are you?" Tutu asked.

Steve stepped into the dimmed light of the cave. "Human. My real name is Steve."

Mos asked, "Not God?"

Steve said, "Mos, I am sorry. I deceived you. I am called a human. The bad men who invaded your village are also humans."

Tutu asked, "Why?"

"Why the bad humans?"

"Why?" He repeated.

"Follow me and we can talk."

"No." Tutu said.

Steve knelt down. "Tutu, the bad humans are still out there looking for us. We are not safe in the tunnel. Follow me into safe shelter and you'll start getting answers."

Tutu hesitated.

Mos said, "I will follow, Go . . . Steve."

Steve stared into the Gemp's eyes. He recognized the look of disappointment, or it could have been a projection of his own feelings of guilt and disappointment. He stood up and walked to the hidden door entrance. Mos, Kiri, Hela, and Feme stood behind him. It took Tutu a few seconds to make up his mind. He followed Steve.

Chapter 10

Codper stood in the middle of the Village. The ground was littered with dead Gemps. A deep satisfaction can over him as he stepped over several little bodies. To his right he heard a female Gemp scream. Then a single shot. Two soldiers walked out from the forest laughing. One of them said "HumanTD", both laughed again. Codper lifted the walkie-talkie to his mouth. "Captain Pierce, report."

Nothing.

"Report!" He clicked the Talk-Button twice. "Has anyone seen the Captain?"

"Sir?"

Codper turned away. "Yes?"

A sergeant stood with his M16 pointed down at the ground. "You ought to see this."

"Lead the way, son."

***

Steve walked through the disguised door. Oscar spotted Hela and Feme and ran to them. They embraced one another.

Oscar signed, "Glad you are safe and here."

Hela said and signed, "Elder, explain what has happened."

Grenier stepped into the light. He waited for Tutu, Mos, and Kiri to enter. The heavy door clicked shut. "I can explain."

All the Gemps turned to Grenier.

"Strange, I know. But if you can give me a few moments you will have some answers. Follow me." Grenier lead them into an adjacent room.

***

The Sergeant took Codper through a path of broken low hanging tree branches. Even before the Colonel reached the spot he smelled death. "Damn!" He said as he saw Captain Pierce sitting up against a tree. His rifle's barrel rested against his right thigh, the rest of the gun between his legs.

Codper knelt down and noticed the wound in his chest. Must have had it on auto when it went off he thought. Then he looked down and saw Pierce's blood soaked crotch. "What happened?" Codper asked, but he felt he knew. Suicide?

"Not sure, sir. One of the Gemps, maybe?" The Sergeant had a sense of what happened, too.

Both men looked at each other. Codper blushed deep red, the Sergeant a shade lighter.

"Sir?"

Codper stood up. "Is the Lieutenant nearby?"

"He was chasing down some Gemps last report over the radio."

"Find him. We need to get Grenier and the others to pull this off. Start checking the outposts."

The sergeant saluted, turned, and walked away.

***

Grenier sat in one of the chairs. "Please have a sit."

The Gemps looked at one another.

Grenier said, "It hasn't been that long since you sat in a chair."

They hesitated.

Oscar pulled out a chair for Hela and Feme. He sat in a chair next to the two.

Hela sat first, then Feme, both looking like small adults in a large playroom for giants.

Tutu sat next. He jumped over the armrest and planted his bottom solidly on the chair seat.

Mos lifted himself up cautiously. He had a look on his face as if he remembered something. He looked over to Kiri, who was seated next to him. She nodded and recognized his expression. She, too, remembered something familiar about a table and chair.

Grenier cleared his throat. "Thank you. My name is Grenier. First, I have to apologize. You may not remember this, but not too long ago you sat in chairs like these. You sat at a table and listened to a human, standing in front of the room like this one, teach you how to talk. A human taught you how to eat, cook, make bows and arrows. A human taught you how to . . . "

Tutu yelled, "Enough!"

Grenier sat quietly, but he did not avoid eye contact with Tutu.

After a moment Tutu looked away, "I not believe you."

Grenier nodded. "Fair enough. I'll be right back." He walked out of the room for a moment. He returned with a remote control in his hand. "I'd like to show you something then."

Tutu watched the human as he moved his thumb across a small black strip of wood. A large white cloth came down from the top of the ceiling. "What is this?" He hissed.

Grenier ignored him for the moment. He thought, 'this is theater, my suspicious friend' and smiled.

Tutu looked across the room at the others. He

was uncertain as how to act. Should he just attack the humans? Or wait. Then he remembered how Elder and Not God now Steve fought off the dirty Gemps. The screams they made. The death they created. He would wait.

Grenier press his thumb on the small bit of wood. The lights dimmed and a projector dropped from the ceiling. "What you are about to see is moving mind images projected onto this white cloth. It's not magic. It is called technology. So, please do not be afraid." He pressed the play button.

A large human face appeared on the screen. Feme jumped and screamed. Oscar jumped over to her chair. He hugged and cooed. Tutu and Hela hissed at the face. Only Mos and Kiri remained silent.

Kiri frowned. She remembered something about the face. It was comforting and caring and happy.

Mos looked over to Kiri. He frowned, too. "Mary?"

Kiri turned her head to face Mos. She nodded.

Grenier said, "Mary Austin is her name. She was one of many caregivers who worked the farm."

Tutu walked over to the screen and peeked behind it.

Grenier paused the video. He would wait.

Mos and the others walked over to Tutu.

"No one is here?" Tutu said.

"It is a projection. An image of the person. Like looking into the lake except we can show the image many times, anytime."

"No one is here?" Tutu repeated.

Mos said, "No one is here."

Hela said, "No one is here."

Feme said, "No one is here."

Kiri said, "No one is here."

The Gemps circled the projector screen several times crossing in front of the light.

Grenier waited patiently. He liked what he saw.

Steve watched with fascination as the Gemps inspected the screen. A few moments later Tutu grabbed a chair and started scrutinizing the projector. He found the keypad controls and pressed a red button. The projector powered off.

Oscar bantered and moved over to Steve.

Steve smoothed Oscar's hair as the little chimp's teeth clicked.

Grenier pressed the on button.

Tutu and the other Gemps jumped. Tutu pressed the red button again. The projector blinked out.

Grenier pressed the on switch.

Tutu pressed the red button.

Lights on, lights off, lights on, lights off, light on.

Mos said, "Tutu. Grenier turns thing . . ."

"Projector." Grenier interrupted.

". . . projector by small piece of wood he is holding."

Tutu walked over to Grenier.

Grenier moved the control away as Tutu tried to snatch it from his hand.

Tutu hissed.

Grenier, taking his cue from Steve, hissed back and louder.

Tutu hadn't expected that. He remembered Grenier dishing out his own brand of death on the wild Gemps. He backed down.

Grenier said, "Ask me nicely and I'll give it to you."

Tutu stared.

Grenier stared back.

Tutu blinked first, "I changed my mind."

"All right by me, but I would like you to sit back down in the chair so that I may continue."

Tutu stood his ground.

"You wanted answer, yes?" Grenier said.

Tutu nodded.

"Then please sit back down."

The Gemp stood fast.

"Please, Tutu. Answers. Promise."

Tutu frowned and walked back to his chair. He sat in a huff. The others were already seated. The large human face was still on the screen. "Mary."

Grenier continued, "She was one of your caregivers." He resumed the video.

Mary said, "Hi!" She stepped back to show a thin blonde hair young woman with a bright smile. Her hair was tied back with a pink bow. She wore bright pink spandex pants and a green cotton top that was partly covered by a long white lab coat. When she talked she seemed to bubble and gush. "Welcome to the Farm. My name is Mary and I'll be your host." She giggled.

The Camera followed Mary throughout the tour. It stopped and focused on a group of very young looking Gemps. Tutu was standing over a young Mos and Kiri.

Young Tutu was angry and yelling at the two, "My toy! My toy! My toy!"

Mary ran over and rubbed Tutu's chest. "Yes Tutu, your toy, but you can share. It will always be your toy until you decide to give it away. But, right now you are sharing."

"My toy!"

She smoothed his head and said, "Strong Tutu, your toy."

"My toy!"

Mary changed her voice, "Tutu!"

He was startled and looked her in the eyes, "Brave, strong, wise Gemps share. Your toy, but you like to share."

He nodded and relaxed. "Tutu will share."

The scene changed. Hela and Feme were playing with blocks of wood. Oscar walked over, sat next to the two. Kissed each one on the cheek, knocked the blocks over and ran. Feme and Hela chased Oscar, knocking things over, laughing and screaming. Steve appeared.

"Oscar!"

Oscar playfully screamed while being chased. He ran into Steve knocking him down. Hela and Feme stepped on Steve as they followed.

The scene changed again. A room filled with Gemps seated behind desks were listening to Kelly recite the alphabet.

Another change. Grenier is staring into the camera. He is holding it. "Hopefully we're onto two stage by the time you see this. I am sorry. But if you are seeing this video I apologize again. You don't-didn't believe me. You don't-didn't remember who I am. You don't remember Steve, Kelly, or when you first met Oscar. Making you forget was necessary. Now it is necessary you believe and we move on. Enjoy your new freedom. This is where life will get exciting and you have a purpose. Learn everything . . ." A young Tutu snatches the camera. "Learn learn

learn learn learn." Grenier gets control of the camera again. He's relaxed and smiling. "Until then."

A collage of different scenes played on the screen. A few minutes later the video ended.

Grenier turned on the light.

Mos stared at Steve. "I don't remember, not God anymore but now is Steve."

Steve nodded, "You will, in time, but now you'll have a whole new world of learning ahead of you. You'll see things as I and Oscar Elder sees them. You'll . . ."

"I am mad." Tutu said.

Grenier nodded. "I know."

"I am mad at you and the other humans."

Grenier nodded again. "I understand. But I need your help now."

"No help."

"I will help." Mos spoke up.

Kiri added, "Mos help, I help."

Feme and Hela nodded.

Tutu asked, "Why would I help?"

"Brave, strong, wise Gemps help. That's why."

Tutu's face relaxed after a second. He nodded. "Tutu will help."

Grenier smiled. Damn that conditioning was strong.

Chapter 11

Codper had a large map of the Island spread across the hood of a Humvee. A dozen locations were circled in an odd misshapen circle.

A walkie-talkie chirped several times.

Codper grabbed it, "Alpha-base, ready."

The voice crackled several times, "Outpost four and five are negative. Moving to post seven. Post one and twelve last. Over."

Codper X'ed out the circles marked four and five on the map. Seven, one, and twelve were left.

***

Grenier held up a handgun that was converted to shooting tranquilizer darts. "This is called a magazine and it holds six darts." He pulled a bullet out from the magazine. "This thin covering breaks away the moment the bullet leaves the barrel." He pointed to the front end on the gun. "You squeeze the trigger toward you to fire the gun. The gun will kick a little, so you have to hold it firmly in your hand." He placed the magazine into the pistol grip. Slide back on the barrel and let it slide forward. He took the gun off safety, aimed at the far wall of the storage room and squeezed the trigger.

Tutu and the others jumped from the gun's bark.

"Outside the gun won't sound as loud." He walked over to a black chest marked 'weapon accessories' and opened it. He pulled out plastic eye protectors and headphones for the Gemps. The humans got earplugs.

Steve and Kelly helped Oscar and the Gemps with their headphones.

"Tutu, you first. I want to show you how to fire this gun."

Tutu slowly walked over. He understood that squeezing the trigger made it bark, but he was still apprehensive enough to eye it cautiously.

Grenier positioned Tutu with the gun in his hands.

"Tutu, place your index finger here along the barrel." He tapped Tutu's index finger. "Get a firm grip. It will jump out of your hands if you hold it too lightly." He made sure Tutu had a firm grip. "Place the tip of your index finger on the trigger." He had to push the finger tip over the trigger. "Pull the tip of your index finger toward . . ."

BANG!!!

Tutu nearly dropped the gun.

"Very good. Do it again."

Bang!!!

Tutu did not jump as dramatic as before.

"Better. Fire again."

Bang.

Grenier nodded. "Fire again, but this time on your own."

Tutu did and he liked it.

Grenier went through the steps with the other Gemps.

Feme dropped the weapon once.

Mos dropped it three times.

Kiri and Hela fired the weapon like pros.

Grenier, satisfied the Gemps could fire the weapon without killing themselves, moved to the next stage. Teaching them how to aim and to safely carry the gun. Reloading was last.

One hour later Grenier decided it was time to break. All his Gemps learned at a phenomenal rate. They all had excellent eyesight and aimed with deadly accuracy.

"Time to eat." Grenier said. He walked over to a storage box marked MREs. Pulled a dozen out and handed a pack to each person. He ripped the top off with his teeth and spilled the contents onto the conference table. The Gemps mimicked him.

Steve opened Oscar's.

Fast learners Grenier told himself. Very fast. Almost too fast. As everyone ate he got up and walked over to the weapon's accessory box. He pulled out communication earpieces. He tapped on a small button on the side of each comm-piece. Only one needed a new battery. He walked over to the table and handed everyone an earpiece, including Oscar. "Tapped this button to turn it on. Tap it again to turn it off. Tap this button to change how loud the talking is."

Mos said, "Loud?"

Grenier nodded. He tapped his piece on and placed it in his right ear. The back wrap hooked nicely over his ear. He positioned the mike close to his mouth.

Mos did the same thing.

"Can you hear me?"

Mos ripped the piece away from his ear.

"That is loud. Tapped this button to make the noise softer."

Mos put the piece back on and tapped the volume button.

"How is this?" Grenier asked.

Mos had the volume down to 2. "Does not hurt. Sound normal like you are next to me."

Grenier nodded. Quick study. "Alright everyone. Place your comm-pieces on and adjust the volume."

Kelly helped Oscar with his comm-piece.

The chimp grunted several times and moved his mouth like he was talking.

Steve scratched the top of his head.

"Now that we have been fed, can safely shot our weapons, and have communication here is what we are going to do." He looked around at the stern expressions around him. "We are outnumbered and out gunned. But we have the element of surprise on our side. The bad humans think we can't fight back. We can and we will. I'll make this plan simple. We shoot as many of them as we can. Go for the arms, stomach, and legs, please. Not the head."

Kiri asked, "Will they be dead?"

"If you shoot the head, yes. But we want them to fall asleep. That's what the bullets do. They are special bullets. The bad humans have to be punished. Killing them is not a punishment."

"Sleeping is not a punishment." Tutu responded.

"True, but when they wake up they will be put into a cage for a very long time. They will not be able to walk freely or see the sun or the moon. The cage is a little bigger than your shelter."

Hela and Feme gasped. "That is bad."

The proximity alarm went off.

Chapter 12

Codper stared at the cave entrance through binoculars. His Humvee was about 50 yards away hidden by several trees. He sent five soldiers to the cave opening as advance guard and another six to the back entrance. He knew there was a third entrance but it was unmarked. In passing some time ago, Grenier told him it was on top of a hill.

Grenier sat at the command station and checked the displays. Two soldiers slowly made their way to the front of the cave. Three soldiers can up to the rear entrance. None on the mountain top or the jungle entrance. He remembered telling the Colonel about the hill top entrance but not the one deep in the jungle. "Steve, Kelly, you two set?"

They both nodded.

Grenier turned to his small band of soldiers. "Remember, avoid head shots. Tutu, you lead. Steve and Kelly will be our eyes. They'll help as best they can from inside. Feme, you take the rear. Oscar you keep soldiers busy."

Oscar grinned teeth and signed, "Busy." He made a "B" with his right hand and bumped its wrist against the wrist of his left hand several times.

His Gemps. Grenier took a deep breath. His Gemps. Chances were good that they could come out of this alive. Though they had about two hours training they took to handling weapons and communication gear at a scary fast pace. Uncle Sam got his monies worth.

Codper watched as his advance guard disappeared through the cave entrance. His walkie-talkie crackled. "Entrance cleared." A minute later, "Rear entrance cleared."

Tutu stepped out of the exit first. It was a disguised rotting tree trunk centered amongst a cluster of tall leafy trees. One by one the Gemps slowly slipped out of the hole with Grenier taking up the rear. He had to improvise a LBE harness and belt for the Gemps at the last minute, but the look was impressive. They all wore goggled eye protection, a communications earpiece, the LBE and belt. They all held their weapons pointing to the ground, as instructed, trigger index finger on the barrel, safety on. Each Gemp demonstrated they could click the safety off, effortlessly, before squeezing the trigger.

Codper listened to the comm chatter. All doors accept one had the access code changed. Codper lifted the binoculars to his eyes and started scanning all the mountain tops. Oscar popped out of one. He checked his map. The chimp was about 60 yards from the cave entrance. He picked up his walkie-talkie. "Golf-one, mountain three, about 50 meters, chimp." He waited a second.

The walkie-talkie crackled, "Alpha-one, target spotted."

Codper watched, through his binoculars, Oscar rocking back and forth. Nasty beast he thought. Hope he hits you first shot. He counted to three when he saw the chimp flinch. He was so close.

A nearby rock exploded inches from Oscar's

feet. The little chimp disappeared down the backside of the mountain. "Golf-one, maintain visual on spot. Shoot at your discretion, out."

Tutu signaled the other Gemps to fan out. Mos and Kiri took right with Hela and Feme taking left. Grenier checked their six. He heard Steve's voice on the comm. "Bad guys about 50 feet forward and left of G-1."

Tutu stopped and scanned the area toward his left. He saw movement crossing in front of him. He moved three steps to his left and saw a soldier walking toward the cave entrance. He heard a shot and paused.

Kelly said over the comm, "Miss. Sniper tried for Oscar."

Tutu took another step forward and to his left, clicked the gun off safe, and aimed. He controlled his breathing as Grenier instructed and squeezed the trigger. The gun barked loudly but the dart hit the mark.

The soldier's right arm jerked wildly away from his body. A second later he collapsed.

Tutu smiled. A flood of hormones hit the young Gemp. He had a hard-on.

Codper heard several shots. All of which did not sound like M-16 rounds. He clicked the walkie-talkie talk button several times. "All teams, report in."

"Team six." Crackled in.

"Team 10." Came next.

"Team five."

"Team . . ." A gun barked through the tiny speakers.

Codper said, "Fuck!" He pulled his sidearm out and stepped away from the Humvee.

Grenier made his way to an area that had a good vantage point. He spotted two soldiers hiding in the foliage. Amateurs he thought as he aimed his pistol and barked out a round for each. Grenier moved further into the bush. He checked his six and saw movement. He was being shadowed. Stepping to the right he squatted down behind a tree. His shadow stopped a moment then moved to the left. He heard, "G-0, I'm to your left." He peeked around the tree and saw Mos with Kiri moving toward the Humvee. "Roger that. I see you."

Mos spotted Grenier first. He signed to Kiri, "Over there, G-0."

She nodded and followed Mos.

Both had been about twenty feet from Grenier when they saw him aim his pistol and double tap his trigger. He moved another six feet when he stopped for several seconds. He looked back and darted behind a tree. The two moved left of his position and transmitted they were near.

Kiri noticed that Grenier let out a slight sigh.

Oscar scampered down the side of the mountain after a small rock exploded near his feet. He made his way to the jungle floor and worked his way to the Humvee. He never liked the Colonel. Steve said he could bite him now and that was what he was going to do. A real nasty bite. One that would show blood, maybe bone. Oscar was happy with that thought. Very happy.

Codper thought he heard a twig snap. Two more teams stopped reporting and now he was worried.

Oscar had worked his way through the jungle around the long way to the Humvee. He could smell the Colonel's fear. It was thick and sour.

Codper turned around and saw the little chimp seconds before it leaped at him.

Tutu had taken out several other soldiers. The thrill of hunting Humans was almost too much. It was like a high he had never felt before. It was better than sex and the buildup was unbelievable.

Grenier had followed Mos and Kiri. Intuitively, the Gemps understood that Codper was the head of the snake. They moved through the jungle bush quickly, almost like they were borne from the land. It was uncanny he thought. Hours ago they feared God.

Now they instilled the fear of God. If only he had the Gemps during Iraq and Afghanistan.

Mos and Kiri moved quickly through the bush. Grenier was behind them, but at a distance. Mos knew the human was capable of keeping up at this pace. Any faster and he would be further behind, out of sight. As Mos gave a quick side glance to Kiri he heard Steve's voice over the radio.

"Oscar just jumped the Colonel . . ."

Then he heard a distant gunshot.

"Oscar's down," Steve said. "Don't know how bad. Someone hurry!"

Tutu heard the shot and picked up his pace. The Elder down he thought. The bad human was going to hurt for this one.

Mos emerged from the jungle line in time to see Tutu on the other side of the Humvee. Codper had his left hand over what was left of his ear. His entire left side bloodied with a remnant of the ear exposed. Oscar bite through the cartilage and for that Codper shot him.

Codper screamed, "You fuckin' Monkey!

Oscar slowly got up holding his right arm. It was a flesh wound but deep enough to matter. He hissed at the Colonel.

Codper aimed his pistol. This time he thought, this time you die you piece of shit goddamn fuckin' little beast. I hate you.

Tutu aimed his pistol and squeezed off a round. Grenier said no headshots. Tutu didn't obey.

The round struck Codper just behind the right ear. It shattered and knocked Codper to the ground unconscious. Unfortunately, the slow velocity bullet hit bone and disintegrated without penetrating. Codper would live.

Grenier wished he had been faster. When he entered the clearing it had already been too late. Codper was face down in the dirt. He walked over and felt for a pulse. The bastard was still alive. Pity. He resisted the urge to double tap some rounds into the back of his head, but the bastard needed to face military justice. He needed to spend life in a prison making big rocks out of little rocks until the day his ghost left his miserable pathetic hypocritical body. So much pain and suffering this one man caused. All for a belief. Grenier did what he thought a fitting punishment on his part. He spat in the Colonel's unconscious face. "Bastard," he said, backed up ten feet from the Colonel and shot him in the leg. He then picked up the walkie-talkie. "This is Colonel Grenier. Lieutenant Colonel Codper has been incapacitated. A SEAL team has been dispatched to assist us and will arrive soon. You get one chance to surrender. This is it. I will not be making a second offer. Colonel out." He placed the walkie-talkie in his pocket and turned around. His Gemps had assembled around him. Oscar was between Hela and Feme. They were smoothing his head and making him feel better. Grenier's Gemps he thought. God help this world now.

The End

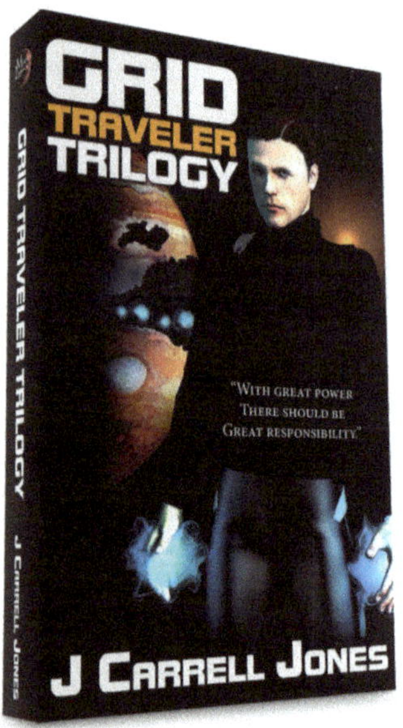

Available online, at your local
book store, or from
http://mythicallegends.com

Forget Star Wars, Forget Star Trek
The DARKSIDE TRILOGY
Is the Sci-Fi Saga of the New Millennium

A Tale Born of the
Headlines of Today

DISCOVERY
VOLUME I OF THE DARKSIDE
WILLIAM HAYASHI

CONCEPTION
VOLUME 2 OF THE DARKSIDE TRILOGY
WILLIAM HAYA

CONFRONTATION
VOLUME 3 OF THE DARKSIDE TRILOGY
WILLIAM HAYASHI

Available at
Amazon.com and
Barnes & Noble

EXTRASOLAR
J. Ryan Malone 2011

GRID TRAVELER SERIES
LINES CROSSED
MAGICK
THE BURDEN I MUST CARRY
FOR MYSELF
AND FOR HUMANITY
- CAPTAIN SEAN BLAKEMORE
THE MOST HIGH GODDESS

The Darker Side

Tonya R. Moore

Claude dreamed that he was back in the old rainforest. He dreamed that he was surrounded by the blanketing moss that crept out of the dark, crawled over wood and swept across the earth under his feet. He dreamed of his dead twin. He dreamed that her lifeless body was still sprawled half-in, half-out of the shallow end of the river, the soaked hem of her red summer dress bobbing in the inky wet. There was a noise, an awful noise that came rushing into his head. That strange sound followed him down and back up the old road, in and out of dreaming.

Jolting wide awake, he squeezed his eyes shut against sunlight streaming in through the cracks in a wooden window. He frowned up at the soot-clouded ceiling of the shack that he and Caroline Dewitt, an ex-student of his father, had taken shelter in during the night.

Then he remembered where he was: Cockpit Country, Jamaica, a lush expanse riddled with limestone sinkholes, snaky rivers and hoary caves. The terrain was treacherous. This was a land where ancient gods and demons once roamed, a place shrouded in secrets and myths. For Claude, the dark heart of this Caribbean jewel was the stuff of nightmares but this time, he hadn't just been dreaming.

He'd really come back to this godforsaken place. For the next few minutes, all he could do was lay there trying his damnedest to remember what the hell had possessed him to do a thing like that.

Caroline was already awake beside him. She sat halfway unsheathed from her sleeping bag, fiddling with the thick braid into which she'd gathered her hair. How long had she been sitting there watching him, catty eyes lit up with avid curiosity?

"I really wish you wouldn't do that," he muttered. "It's creepy."

"What were you dreaming about?" She asked, blatantly ignoring his complaint.

Caroline had a thick, lyrical voice, which she'd laughingly credited to her West African ancestry the day before. It seemed a strange assertion coming from one he'd heard locals call a coolie. Her eerily feline eyes bored into his now, searching. It was as if she expected his answer to have some deeply profound meaning.

He didn't answer.

"Fine," her fingers stopped working briefly. "Don't tell me."

Claude doubted the academic had any real intention of leaving it at that. Her clinical interest and insight were unnerving, left him feeling that she could see things he didn't want her to see, didn't want anyone to see. He didn't like it. Not one bit.

"I keep having these dreams," he finally said. "I'm always dreaming about this place. It's like there's something important I forgot. And I've been hearing this… sound."

"What kind of sound?" Caroline asked, as if nothing else he said was of any consequence.

"I don't know. A noise."

Unexpectedly, the academic seemed satisfied with that answer. She tugged on her sneakers and fussed with the laces. "What are we doing about breakfast? I brought bun and cheese. I could maybe scare up a granola bar if you'd rather skip the local fare."

Claude wondered whether bun and cheese was really all she'd brought or if she was just amusing herself at his expense again. "There's canned fruit and soup in my backpack," he offered.

"Fruit and soup…." She made a beeline for the doorway, chuckling for reasons known only to herself.

"Claude!" Her panicked yelp had him bolting right out of his sleeping bag. "Claude, get out here!"

He stepped into the unforgiving morning

light. Someone had left quite the grisly gift on the doorstep. An indigo and yellow snake had been killed, chopped into eight pieces. Its head had been piked onto a rusty-bladed machete and the crude tool jammed into the hard earth. The ground around the big nanka's carcass was sprinkled with vivid, red spider lilies.

His eyes settled on one of the hapless blossoms. Was someone else here? Was there someone following and watching their every move?

"Do you know what it means?" Caroline asked, sounding strained. "I know the people here, but I don't know about this."

Claude met her worried gaze with kind of a wry half-smile half-grimace. "Guess I'm just not welcome here."

Not like he needed to be told. He didn't realize that he was biting down on his bottom lip until he tasted blood. He'd gone numb, couldn't even feel it.

He bent, grasped the machete by the handle and yanked it up, out of the dirt. He pointed the tip at the spider lilies. "Where do these things grow?"

Caroline hesitated. "Why?"

"They were Tarah's favorite," Claude frowned down at the bloodied blade. "There's no deeper reason." Not for him, and he got the feeling, not for the one who'd left it at the doorstep either.

Caroline pointed vaguely north-westward. "Roughly a quarter mile on. There's a whole field of them. They bloom there all year round. Strange thing. They're not even indigenous."

"Thanks," he turned to go back inside. "I can pretty much figure where I'll need to go from here. You can just wait here, right?"

"Kelvin told me about what happened here when you were a kid," Caroline said suddenly. "About your sister, the way she went missing."

"Yeah," he stopped, back still turned to her. "What about it?"

"Nothing," she murmured. "Never mind."

Tarah had died. She'd drowned in the river, deep in these hills. There was no use in talking about it.

He found the field east of the main river, where the spider lilies thrived in abundance. He'd brought the bloody machete that had been left at the doorstep that morning. He chopped off enough of their red little heads to fill the bamboo bucket. He waded to the deep end of the fiery flower-sea.

A path to the place where his twin had died was hidden by bramble and brush, but he found it easily. Even if he'd been blindfolded, he would have found it as effortlessly. He stood at the foot of the slippery steps carved into the steep mountain slope. Those steps must have been there for centuries before Claude first climbed them as a teen. He doubted anyone in this country even remembered who had carved them anymore. From there he ascended into the thick of the hills.

The way was obscured by morning mist and the crush of trees. Halfway to the top, Claude stopped. He turned. Seeing no one there, he released a shaky breath. A second ago, he'd been so certain there was someone behind him. Would being right have made him less uneasy? The mountain had gone silent, save for the sound of the wind spiraling down through the trees and a waterfall's distant thunder. Claude continued. His grip on the machete tightened. He couldn't shake the feeling that something or someone was watching his every move.

The ancient steps led to an arced tunnel carved into the karst near the summit. Claude stepped into the darkness and was thrust into daylight on the other side of the slope. Vertigo grabbed hold. The steps continued steeply downward. The thick foliage downslope obscured his view of the river, but he could see the radical divide where the verdant valley was split into extremes of day and night.

On the darker side, the woods were blackened by what he was inexplicably convinced had to be something far more fearsome than the shadow of the next ridge. The air was swollen with the cries of birds in the wild, the roars of scattered cascades and gurgling rills. Brimming with trepidation, he descended into the seething maw of the hollow.

By the time reached the bottom, his guts were all knotted up inside. He couldn't shake that sick feeling. Slivers of that awful day kept battering at his splintered memory.

As the world around him tilted. Tarah had floated to the surface as if unseen hands were raising her body up from the deep. Claude remembered with stark clarity, her lifeless body bobbing in the water. That image burned brightly in his memory, tormenting him endlessly. There were gaps in his memory. The crucial moments before and immediately after his sister's death escaped him completely. Something terrible had happened. Something so terrible he couldn't even remember.

Tarah had been in the river, but Claude couldn't recall pulling her from the water. He could only remember seeing her lying there against the bank, still partially submerged. He remembered kneeling beside her body, pressing his lips against the dead flesh. He remembered how cold she was, like she'd sunk deep into the depths and stayed down there for days before slowly rising back up to the top.

Here he was now, after all this time. Boot heels sinking down into the slippery soft mud, he cast Tarah's favorite flowers into the murky water. He watched their slow procession into the vein of the river where they were swallowed up by the dark.

What was he doing? Tarah was long gone and she wasn't coming back. What the hell was he doing here after all this time?

He saw it then, that thing.

The tall, shadowy figure stood upright, expelling air in ragged breaths. It stepped closer to the river's edge. Claude's eyes went wide. No way was that human! The horrible realization made his body tremble. The beastly body was completely covered in the breathing moss that grew on everything. It crouched there, the white of its wide eyes spearing across the small distance between them. It flashed Claude a toothy grimace. Had it had smiled or simply bared its teeth? It crouched there watching him, watching him and watching him.

"You!" An indescribable rage bubbled forth. Claude glared into the eyes of his ancient foe. Somehow, he found his voice. "It was you, wasn't it?" he pointed. "You killed her!" His grip on the handle of the machete tightened. "You're the one!"

Brandishing the large blade, he dashed forward into the river. The backlash was instantaneous. Some unseen forced knocked him backward, sent him flying. His back slammed into the muddy riverbank. The world tilted, went dark. Claude let out a choked cry as pain lanced through his right leg. Something was broken. He was on the ground and broken. He couldn't seem to remember how he'd gotten that way. His vision kept going blurry. He heard footsteps, and then the monster was looming over him. He flailed, tried to scramble away, but couldn't. He reached blindly for the machete—anything!

He heard it again, that strangely ominous sound. That awful noise was like a train hurtling by. The earth beneath him shuddered like it was being torn apart from deep inside.

The creature crouched low. The scent of green and rot became overpowering. Pain radiated through every cell in Claude's body. He couldn't move, could barely even breathe. His eyes failed him. Helpless and terrified, he waited for the fatal blow but the gruesome attack never came. He felt something light and wet fall on his chest. It happened again. It took him a while to realize that they were the flowers he'd thrown into the river, every last one of them.

As Claude lay there stunned, the dark body backed away. The mad noise that filled his head was receding. He heard brambles breaking as the strange one retreated, plunging into the arms of the darker side of the river. It slowly became easier to breathe. Lightheaded, Claude struggled to keep his grasp on consciousness.

When he came to, Caroline was with him. She was seated on the muddy ground beside him with her knees drawn up to her chin.

He tried to move. Pain radiated through every cell in his body. He bit down on a hoarse yelp.

"Keep still," Caroline ordered. "I called for help but they'll be a while and I don't know how badly you were hurt."

"I told you not to come," Claude croaked but he was grateful for her presence.

She'd bandaged his leg with a section of her shirt, using skinny limbs from a nearby tree as a splint for his leg. The rest, she'd used on her own hand. There was blood soaking through the fabric wrapped around the space between her forefinger and thumb.

She noticed where he was looking. "Nothing serious. I just got a bit careless."

"Caroline."

"What happened?" She drilled. "You didn't come back down, so I followed even though you didn't want me to. Good thing I--"

"Did you see it?" he demanded, still dazed.

Caroline's brow furrowed. "See what?"

"That thing!" He bit out impatiently. "It was here. It was right here. I thought it was going to kill me but it didn't." He looked to his companion helplessly. "I don't know why it didn't."

Caroline's expression was odd but she only shook her head. "If there was something here, it was gone by the time I came."

The tributary had widened. Because of the quake, the water was frothing and ruddy from the topsoil that had tumbled over the bank and spiraling down into a whirlpool. Soon, there would only be a gaping cavity where dark water once flowed.

"I don't get it." he reached out for one of the wilting red flowers. "All it did was give these back to me."

If that thing—whatever it was—had killed his sister, wouldn't it have killed him too? How had Tarah really ended up in the river?

"I couldn't remember. Still can't," he murmured. "What if all I did that day was just stand here and watch her die?"

Caroline was staring at him strangely again.

"What?"

"It's just," her fingers curled into the wet earth. "You keep talking like the day you found Tarah was the day she died."

"Well, yeah. She wanted to show me this really cool place she'd found. We came here." He swallowed, but just couldn't dislodge that painful lump in his throat. "Then everything went to hell."

"I'm telling you, that's not possible." Caroline rummaged around in her backpack. "Claude," she asked. "Know anything about this island's history?"

"Just the textbook stuff."

"This island has seen a lot of death," the scholar explained. "That was long before the likes of Columbus reached the West Indies. The people who lived here his time were the Taino but they weren't the first."

"I know at least that bit," Claude scoffed. "Before that, there were the…?"

"The Ciboney," Caroline supplied with a brief grin. "Before them, the Igneri inhabited the island. Before that—who knows? For a long time, this island's history was a repeating pattern of people settling here, and then vanishing from the face of the earth. It happened again and again. No one knows how long this kept happening, or why."

"Then the Taino settled. You probably know the rest. The Europeans came, bringing disease and slavery. It didn't take long to wipe out the native population. Well," Caroline clarified. "Some managed to escape into these lands."

Claude peered into the darkness across the now raging river. Rampant moss and shadowy foliage masked whatever secrets Cockpit Country kept. What had become of the runaway Taino? What did they find waiting here?

"I don't understand what any of this has to do with my sister," he finally said.

"I looked into it before agreeing to take you here, you know." From her backpack, Caroline produced a worn notebook. She flipped through the pages. "By all accounts—except yours—Tarah went missing. She'd already been missing for three days when you found her body in the river. You say she was with you the whole time but Claude, no one else remembers that. Not Kelvin. Not your mother. I mean no one."

"That's insane!" He shook his head vehemently. "That doesn't even make any sense. I remember. I remember every second of it. She was here. She was—hell." His head hurt. It felt hot inside his skull. It felt wrong, so wrong. "You think I'm just making this up?"

"No," Caroline firmly denied. "I don't think that at all."

"Then what?" He demanded harshly. "Am I going insane?" He asked, and just couldn't dull that bitter edge to his words. "Then maybe my mom isn't the only one who belongs in a--"

"That's not what I'm saying at all." Caroline cut

him off before he could finish that tirade. "I do believe you. I believe it happened. Everything. Just as you said."

"Then what?" Claude didn't know what to think now. "What exactly are you getting at?"

"I've heard a few old stories; they all went down pretty much to the same tune." Caroline stuck the notebook back into her backpack. He was dazzled by the light streaming down and lighting up her liquid-amber irises. "The older locals avoid this area. It's too unnerving for them."

"Ridiculous," Claude muttered. "Do you really expect me to buy into that garbage?"

"Can you deny it?" Caroline challenged. Her fascination and envy were palpable. "Can you honestly deny it, after you've actually lived it?"

Claude's protest died in his throat, as he contemplated the horrifying possibility. For three days—all those years ago--there had been something living and breathing beside him. Something no one else could see.

Had Tarah encountered some forgotten relic of the Tainos' tragic history or was the creature he tried to confront something much more primitive? What about the one who'd led him here in the first place? Had that been his sister or not?

Claude shuddered. "I just can't make any sense of this."

"You don't get to make sense of it," Caroline snorted sympathetically, prying the muddy flower from his trembling fingers. "You just make your peace with it."

Scores of doomed crawfish and river fish writhed and twisted in the thickening mud. This branch of the river was gone, had slipped away through the crack the quake had made in the earth. Gone like Tarah. Gone like the atavic beast that had waited for Claude on the darker side of the river.

Burrowing deep down into the bones of the earth, Black River twisted sinuously through the heart of Cockpit Country.

\#\#\#

A MISSION
OF MERCY
FOR THE ENEMY
OF HER ENEMY
BECOMES A
STRUGGLE
FOR
SURVIVAL
PARANORMAL
ROMANCE

Billy

by Devon Nicholson

Good evening boys, girls and ghouls alike. On All Hallow's eve it is tradition to share stories of fright and terror. On this particular night however, I wish to share with you, not a story of a monster or beast, but one of a boy. His name is Billy. Now Billy is like any good boy. He washes his hands thoroughly, he combs his hair, brushes his teeth daily, and always gives thanks before a meal. Billy kept out of trouble, made sure to listen to his mother, and always be on his very best behavior. He did not like to play with other children, and did not have many friends. Perhaps he was shy? It can be very difficult to make friends at such a young age. No one really knew much about Billy but there was one thing that was always certain. He loved Halloween. He spent the whole year preparing his costume, anticipating the night when he would be able to visit all his wonderful neighbors, and sample one life's sweetest creations; candy. How Billy loved candy. He loved it more than anything in the world. He loved it so much even, that his mother only allowed this one holiday for him to have any. Billy can become rather "excited" when it comes to candy, so she thought it best he take it in very mild doses.

"Billy?" She would say in a very soft and warm tone.

"It's Halloween again. I know you are excited but remember your manners and try to keep out of trouble. Ok?"

"Yes, Mom." He said in utter compliance. Billy truly was a good boy and he knew better than to go against his mother's wishes. With a hug and a kiss Billy bid his mother adieu and set out into the night in search of his most treasured treats.

The streets were alive with activity. All manner of madmen, monsters, witches, demons, and the occasional fairy, littered the streets. The ghoulish decorations created a scene filled with both wonder and terror. All lovingly bathed in the pale moon light. There was a chorus of door bells and the familiar greeting of "Trick or Treat" as bag after bag was filled with paper wrapped decadence. Billy could wait no longer; standing in the street, dressed as marionette, he went to the first house. He rang the door and waited patiently, burlap sack with mouth agape, waiting to receive his reward.

"Trick or Treat" Billy said, swelling with pride.

"Oh my goodness, what a terrifying costume! I love your spirit kid, here's something extra."

The kind stranger gave Billy six pieces of Candy. The young boy thanked the stranger and went off to the next home. What luck? Six on the first house? Billy figured it was just a fluke, but to his surprise each home he visited was more gracious then the next. The guests were taken by the level of detail in his costume. The seemingly self-suspended wooden handle, the way each string reacted in time with his gestures, and his costume clipped and clopped along the pavement from the expertly carved wooden appendages. He was a work of art and he was greatly appreciated by everyone he met…well not everyone. On the way to the final house a trio of older boys tried to harass Billy.

"That's a lot of candy you got there." One of the boys said from behind a cracked hockey mask.

"You gonna eat all that by yourself? Don't you think that's a little selfish?" Another said, inching closer to Billy.

He was beginning to feel rather uncomfortable by the strange boys but he remembered what his mother said. He stood firm and offered them a response.

"You can have some if you'd like. I wouldn't mind sharing."

The boys seem rather unamused by Billy's offer. They had something else in mind.

"How about you just give us the bag?"

"No." Billy said in a very firm tone.

"What did you say?" The roundest of the trio

said, now looking visibly infuriated. He would have laid a hand on Billy but thankfully an adult, watching the event from her front porch, had come to his aid.

The night was getting late and Halloween was drawing to an end. It was time for Billy to head to his favorite spot in town, spill the sugary contents onto the floor, sort, and then eat them one by one. He had a very simple system. First it was the gummies, then the hard candies, a hole in the ground for the unfavorable, and a special spot for the crème de la crème, chocolate. Billy was about to enjoy the first piece when he was suddenly interrupted by a rather unsettling but strangely familiar voice.

"Hello, there little puppet boy. What brings you to our little hang out?"

Poor Billy, he knew who it was that called to him. It was the boy in the mask from before. Billy grabbed his sack and quickly tried to pack his candy and leave but he was stopped short by even more trouble. A stocky hand had grabbed a hold of him.

"What's the rush kid? Didn't you want to share? I figure we'd take you up on that offer." Said a voice, the eldest boy, emerging from the shadows.

"That's quite a stash you got there. How did you manage to score so much? All I got was a lousy pack of nerds." The masked boy said disappointedly.

"…They liked my costume." Billy said lowly, carefully eyeing the larger boy, now unraveling a warhead.

"Hey, check it out fellas. This really is a good costume. How do you get that wooden thing to stay up there like that?" The masked boy said, plucking at one of Billy's many strings. Billy shuddered at the touch.

"What's the matter kid? Why you so jumpy? They're just strings!" The masked boy removed a small knife from his pants pocket and cut one of Billy's strings. Billy let out a terrible scream.

"What the hell is wrong with you kid? You don't like when I do this?!" He cut yet another string. Billy's arm fell limp to his side dand again he screamed.

"Heh, this is kinda fun. Anyone one else want a go at it? How about you Kev?" The masked boy said to a third boy, who'd still been watching from the shadows.

"Yea, I could take a go at it. Hand me the knife."

Kev eyed Billy with an almost sinister gaze. He tapped the blade's edge against each individual string, choosing which one he wanted to sever first. Billy struggled to get away but that bloated arm, with sausage-like fingers held him tightly, while the other stuffed all of his hard earned candy into his suppressor's gaping maw.

"Man this stuff is good." The pig child said between bites.

"Slow down Terry, the kid's got a ton. You don't gotta tear through it all at once. "The masked boy said.

"Well come get it while it's still here Rudd, cause I'm getting while the getting's good. Look he's got some of that chocolate you love."

Billy's head turned to Rudd, his eyes pleading. Anything but the Chocolate, Billy thought to himself. Kev picked up on this distress and grabbed himself a piece.

"You like chocolate huh? Me too." Kev slowly unwrapped the paper casing.

"Nooo! No no no! That's my favorite." Billy pleaded tearfully.

"Shut up!" Kev cut another one of Billy's strings and Billy let out another scream.

"I said shut up! You want this don't you?"

Billy nodded his head and whimpered, eyeing his precious candy.

"Good, then this time…when I cut you, don't scream!" Kev sliced away at another string and Billy screamed yet again, this one now sounding less like one of distress, but of excruciating pain. Billy's body had now gone totally limp save for his one arm that appeared to be dangling on the final string. All the while still oddly suspended by the wooden handle.

"Hey Kev?" Rudd said with a bit of concern in his voice.

"What?"

"Maybe we should stop. You know? It was fun for a while but it's getting late and this kid is starting to weird me out."

"Nah man, I got one more string. What are you

worried about?"

"Look man, I don't know about you but something don't feel right. Just look at that thing. That thing shouldn't keep floating like that right? I mean, how is it staying?" Rudd said, eyeing the handle, perfectly suspended above Billy's limp body.

"How the hell should I know? Let him go Terry. I got one left. He doesn't look like he's going anywhere anyway."

"Alright." Terry said with his mouth full, half of Billy's candy nearly consumed.

Kev traced the blade along the final string, licking his lips in anticipation, taking sick pleasure in Billy's discomfort. He threw the piece of chocolate to Terry. Billy could not move his head but his eyes followed the bar, as Terry salivated, his hot breath ruining that which Billy cherished most. As Terry bit down, Kev sliced Billy's finally string. Billy's arm fell and he lay in a contorted heap on the floor. He let out a blood curdling scream. The three boys tried to shield their ears from the piercing screech that seemed to only increase in volume and pitch. Billy's eyes darted around in his head, spiraling out of control as his mouth remained eerily unhinged, the scream now transitioning to a low hum.

"You see! I told you that kid was weird! What the hell did you do man?!"

"I ain't do shit, let's get out of her-"Kev was interrupted by the sudden sound of carving and the cobbling of wood.

"Kev!"

"What is it now man?"

"Dude?! How the fuck is that thing still floating there?!"

Kev could feel the hairs on his neck riding up as he came to grips with Rudd's observation. There was Billy's handle, suspend, with just a pair of jarring strings hanging from its base, and below it was Billy's now still body. The sound of the cobbling grew more intense as the handle began to sway back and forth rhythmically. Neither of the three boys could move, the gently swaying of the handle seemed to hold them in a trance. As it swayed, so did the strings, which now stretched toward the floor, snaking

around Billy's body. Each string finding its severed partner, and reuniting Billy to the Handle's base. First the arms, raised to the sky, wrists hanging lifelessly. Then the body, his feet still dragging along the floor as he assumed an upright position. Then finally his head, which cocked eerily to the side before a pair of eyes rolled from behind the lids and fixed their gaze on Kev. Billy didn't say a word.

"Kev, I think we should go…now." Said Rudd.

"I agree, Terry?"

Billy turned his gaze to Terry.

"Guys, I…I can't move."

"Stop fucking around Terry, let's go."

"No…guys….I'm serious! I can't feel my legs."

"Terry, I'm not playing with you man!"

"Kev…..look." Kev said with great fear in his voice, pointing toward his friend.

Kev followed the floor with his eyes. Terry was right, he couldn't move, for his legs were tethered to the floor by countless puppet strings. Strings that slowly snaked up his body. Strings that had minds of their own.

"Guys….it hurts."

"Fuck man, I'll get you out!" Kev said in a panic as he fumbled with the knife, trying to free his buddy.

"Oh Shit man, hurry up! " Rudd said in a panic as that horrible cobbling sound grew louder each passing moment.

"I'm trying, I can't cut them."

"Kev…." Terry said now in pain, his head reddening as the blood rushed to his face as the strings continued to constrict his body.

"Hang on Terry, I'm gonna get you out!"

The cobbling now increased in tempo and the strings too increased their stricken. Try as he might, Kev could not cut the coils of Billy's wrath and soon Terry was fully encased. The silk tomb was stained red as the razor thin wires now pierced Terry's tubby flesh. Terry's muffled screams were drowned out by the incessant cobbling. Rudd took off, forgetting his friends, attempting to flee. Billy raised an arm. Wires, like violent tendrils lashed out from all angles. They quickly ensnared Rudd in silk. The last thing Kev saw was his friend, yanked into the air, struggling before being pulled, screaming into the darkness. The cobbling suddenly felt silent. Terry was now alone, with Billy; no longer swaying. His eyes fixed on Kev. Kev brandished his knife, sweating profusely, and arms shaking. Kev was afraid and this made Billy smile. Not because Billy knew his aggressor was without options nor that he was about to exact his vengeance. He knew that Halloween wouldn't be over for a few more hours. He wouldn't let any of them go to waste. There was still time to salvage the night.

The next morning Billy arrived home, his burlap sack full. His mother greeted him at the door.

"Billy, you stayed out all night. You must have had a really good time. You didn't get into trouble did you?"

"Not at all mom!" He said with a smile as his mother embraced him.

"I see you got quite a bit of candy there. You didn't eat it all last night?"

"No mom, but could I please have it for today? I promise I won't save any."

"I know you won't. You are such a good boy. Alright, go on upstairs then."

Billy slung the bag over his back and made his way to his room. It was not his favorite spot but he would still pour the contents of the bag onto the floor, sort, and then eat them one by one. He had a very simple system. First toes in one pile, the fingers in another, the trash bin for any of the unfavorable, and of course the crème de la crème, that one piece of chocolate. He promised he'd finished it all today and he would never dare to go against his mother's wishes. After all, Billy was a good boy. He washed his hands thoroughly, he combed his hair, he brushed his teeth, and he gave thanks before his meal.

###

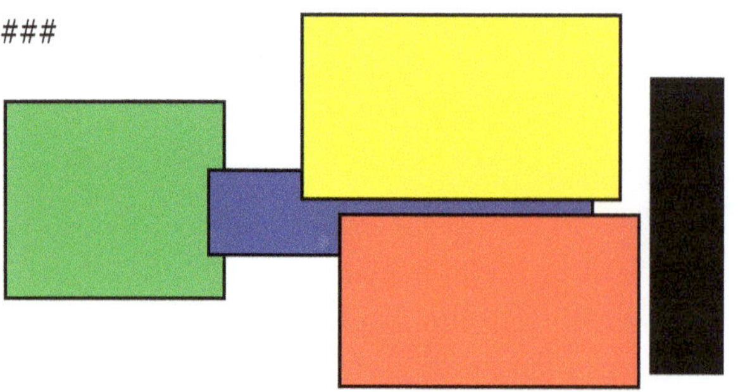

UNTOLD ARE THE THOUGHTS THAT DWELL IN THE SHADOWS OF THE NIGHT. Visit:

http://ariel-x.deviantart.com/

QUEEN BRIGHTLANCE
ON THE SURFACE WE ALL LOOK THE SAME DESTINED TO MARRY BECAME QUEEN INSTEAD
SCI-FI FANTASY

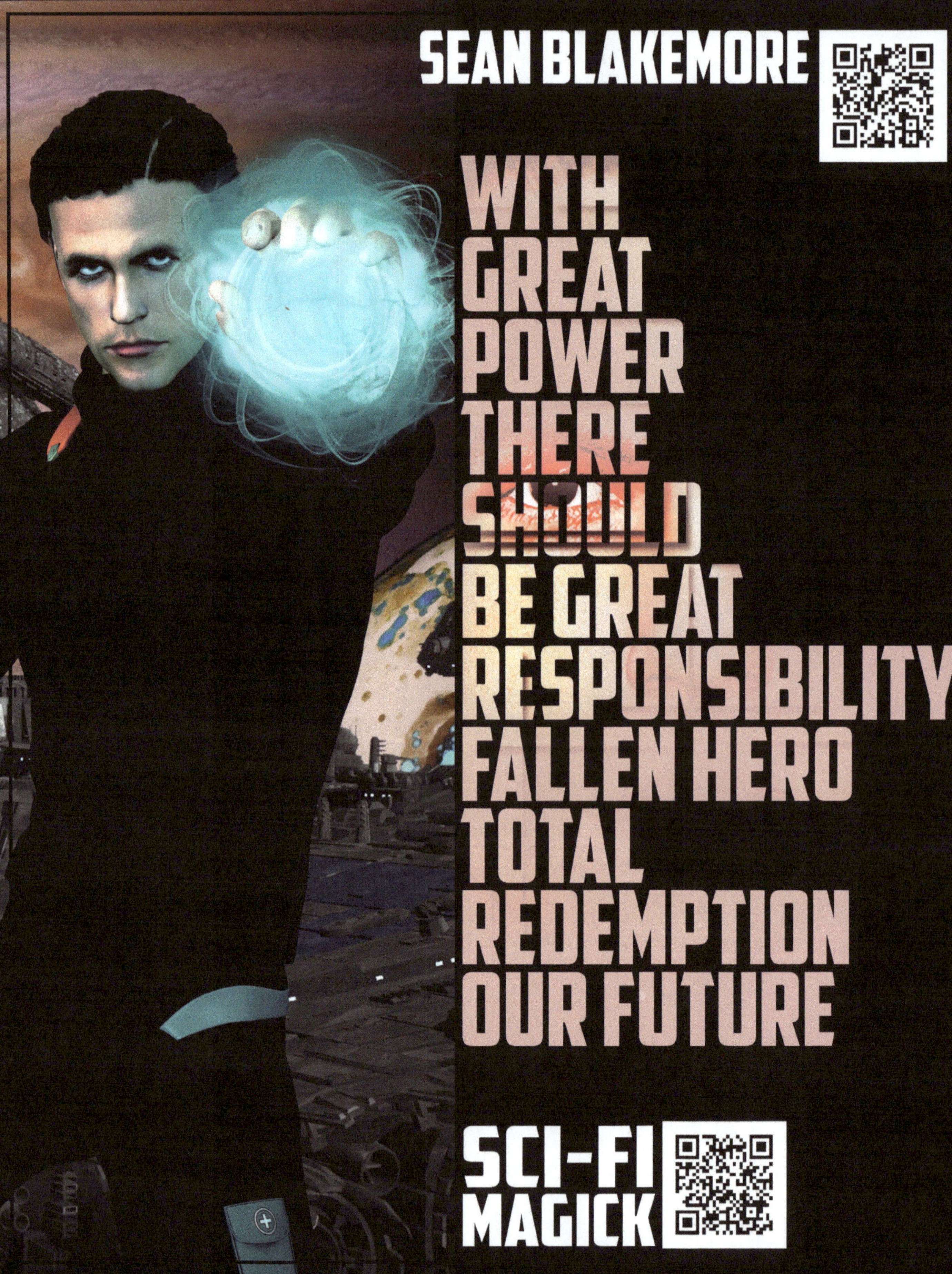

SEAN BLAKEMORE
WITH
GREAT
POWER
THERE
SHOULD
BE GREAT
RESPONSIBILITY
FALLEN HERO
TOTAL
REDEMPTION
OUR FUTURE
SCI-FI
MAGICK

Black Holes and Aspen Summer Snow

Jarita Holbrook

Jeremy Williams was pleased with his presentation on intermediate mass black holes. It was a small audience of thirty people and they had asked very good questions. He didn't expect anything less of the residents of the Astrophysics Institute in Aspen, Colorado.

When he had arrived, the receptionist had greeted him warmly.

"Welcome to the Astrophysics Institute, Dr. Williams…may I call you Jeremy? The Institute hosts week-long workshops throughout the year. While you are here, you are encouraged to share your research with the scientists in residence and build new collaborations."

He found out that most scientists stayed two weeks and brought their families. Jeremy had earned his doctorate in physics with a dissertation topic in astrophysics, and it had taken years of long nights to complete.

The receptionist had asked, "Are you here with your family?"

"No, I work too many hours to have a family."

She had laughed and said, "Well, we encourage working, but Aspen is a unique town with an interesting mining history. I hope you take some time to see some of the sights and experience the local flavor."

Jeremy had found that Aspen was beautiful but very expensive. Fortunately, there were grants to help pay for travel and the housing was subsidized.

When he arrived on Friday the first thing he noticed was the lack of African Americans. Being African American, he was always conscious of when he was the only one or one of few. It was true this week at the Institute as well as far as diversity went; there was a few Chinese, a few Indians, him, and one Latina. That was just the way astrophysics was, still. He didn't mind as long as his colleagues did not discriminate against him.

As the auditorium emptied he shut his laptop and disconnected the projector. A senior scientist approached the podium.

"Hello. I'm Robert Wolfschmidt. I was impressed by your talk. Have you published your results, yet?"

"Dr. Wolfschmidt…it's a pleasure to meet you. No, I've just finished working out the equations before I came here."

"That's great. Why don't we make time to discuss your work in more detail tomorrow? …How does lunch sound?"

Jeremy took a moment to think before answering, "That should be fine."

"Good! See you around here then tomorrow."

"See you then."

Jeremy went back to unplugging his laptop, gathered up his notes and left the auditorium. Both sides of the auditorium had floor to ceiling windows that framed the tall trees that grew on the grounds of the Institute. As he left the building he shook his head in annoyance: the cottonwoods were shedding. It was like snow in the summertime. Under most circumstances it would be beautiful, but the white fluff stuck to his afro. He continually had to brush it off or just look like a dork. Normally he wore a goatee but that just collected fluff as well, so he had shaved it off for while he was in Aspen.

The visiting scientists could be found working on benches out in the sunshine if the fluff didn't bother them. Access to the internet was free and available throughout the facility including in the extensive gardens. Since the town of Aspen was physically small everyone got around on bicycles. The Institute provided bikes that the scientists could rent at a very reasonable price along with helmets and lights. Jeremy took advantage of this and used the opportunity to bike daily at high altitude as a way to stay fit.

Every visitor to the Institute had an office that was shared with another scientist. His officemate was a physicist about fifty years old who was from one of the universities in Chicago and he did his experiments at Fermi Lab. He was pleasant enough and mainly just worked on his laptop. Most of the scientists visiting the Institute were either trying to write their next scientific article or were in the various stages of rewriting and editing; Jeremy's officemate was doing the same. The Institute provided a quiet place free of distractions which allowed the scientists to get caught up on their writing.

Though he had presented on his latest research, Jeremy was trying to finish an article that he had already submitted and had gotten back the referee report. After that article was resubmitted, he planned to write up what he had just presented. After getting feedback from the audience, he knew that his equations were correct and that his results were publishable. Knowing that his research was ready made the whole trip worthwhile and made him grateful to the Institute for inviting him.

He unpacked his laptop and sat down to work for a couple of hours before calling it quits. He managed to address another item on the referee's report. It was a simple error about one of the articles that he had cited. He went back to the article and checked that the page number to which he referred was correct as well as the date of the article. The description that he was using began on one page and ended on the next page. In the draft of his article, he had only cited the first page, so he changed the citation to include both pages.

He was too excited about his latest research to leave it alone. So, he loaded up his presentation from the afternoon and started blocking out its scientific article. He went so far as to write the introduction including the references, before his officemate interrupted him.

"Goodnight, I'll see you tomorrow."

Jeremy answered, "See you then."

He stopped writing, saved his new file, then connected his external drive to do a backup. One of the postdoctoral fellows stuck his head into the office. There seemed be a small group of these younger scientists in the hallway. The postdoctoral fellows, like Jeremy, had their doctorates but were still trying to obtain a coveted faculty position. Being invited to the Institute was prestigious, a good thing to put on a curriculum vita, and could be attractive to potential bosses. The postdocs were excited to be there, but Jeremy could tell that they were intimidated as well.

"Hey Jeremy, nice talk."

"Thank You."

"Yeah, Nice talk!"

Jeremy just smiled.

"We're thinking of going to the Tavern later around 9 o'clock. Do you want to meet us there?"

"Sure. I might be a little late…"

"We will probably be there until late. Just come whenever."

They left and Jeremy listened as their voices got further and further away. He knew that socializing with the other postdocs was important though such socializing tended to be scientifically useless. It wasn't as if he didn't like the other postdocs; just that he tended to take his time making new friends. He made himself be social because any one of them could be in his department in a future position, thus as potential future colleagues Jeremy had a policy of being nice if not friendly. Plus, in this case, he thought it might be good to hang out with people his own age.

Dr. Wolfschmidt appeared at his door. Jeremy startled a bit.

"Sorry, I didn't mean to surprise you."

Jeremy took a calming breath before responding, "No, I just thought the building was empty."

"Oh, there is always someone working all hours. I was just about to go to dinner. I thought maybe we could talk tonight instead of lunch tomorrow?"

"Sure, I was just packing up."

"I'll meet you in the lobby in five minutes."

Jeremy nodded. After packing his backpack, he met Dr Wolfschmidt and they walked to a moderately expensive restaurant to Jeremy's relief. Aspen was really too expensive for his postdoc's salary.

Over dinner, after removing the cottonwood fluff from his hair, Jeremy and Dr. Wolfschmidt talked in detail about his findings about the existence of intermediate mass black holes: They couldn't be seen because astrophysicists were expecting them to appear brightest at shorter wavelengths. In fact, Jeremy found that their electromagnetic flux was distributed such that their radiation peak occurred in both longer wavelength infrared and the expected shorter wavelengths but at the boundary region between ultraviolet and x-ray. Jeremy found that astrophysicists had a bias or maybe a fondness for things that could be seen with the human eye - things that could be seen at optical wavelengths. This bias for the optical was strong enough that if an object couldn't be found in the optical then in some ways it didn't exist so went unreported in favor of those objects that could be verified at optical wavelengths. Given that the objects were black holes, by definition they were not visible in the optical, however astrophysicists expected to see an optical signature from the matter surrounding and falling into the black hole. The shorter wavelength peak was smaller than expected for a black hole because the photons were being reprocessed and output as heat in the infrared. The situation was further complicated because of the lack of instruments that could detect photons at the UV-X-ray transition. Instead, the UV and X-ray flux fitted with a black body curve showed where the peak should be, that integrated with the infrared revealed the energy expected for an intermediate mass black hole.

Jeremy had verified his intermediate black hole candidates by cross-referencing the x-ray, UV, and infrared signatures in this way. Jeremy talked about example after example of the dual peaked objects that incorporated the redistributed black body signature of intermediate black holes. Dr. Wolfschmidt was engrossed enough that he began to take notes. He peppered Jeremy with questions. When it was time for dessert, Jeremy was talked out and made his excuses. With a handshake they parted ways and Jeremy began to walk to his lodgings but remembered the postdoc get together. He wasn't far from the place where they were drinking so decided to make a quick stop.

"Hey, Jeremy. Were you working all this time?"

It took Jeremy a moment to remember the postdoc's name. He took his time wracking his brain for his name while brushing his hair making sure it was free of fluff before saying,

"Hey, Sam. No, I had dinner with Dr. Wolfschmidt."

Sam stiffened, "Don't tell me...he was asking all sorts of questions about your research?"

"Yeah, it was really amazing how much he understood the details. He made me really think about some of my assumptions…"

Jeremy stopped speaking as Sam suddenly bent over grabbing his head and groaning.

"What is it? Are you alright?"

"Damn it! I meant to warn you…"

"Warn me about what?"

"Dr. Wolfschmidt has a history of scooping people…"

Jeremy's stomach dropped. The flattery, the attention, he couldn't believe it. Scooping meant that it had all been just to steal his work.

"What?"

"Yeah, I hope you didn't tell him too much because guaranteed if you did, you will see it in print under his name before you can get it submitted."

Jeremy didn't know if this was some ploy to make him feel bad because Sam was jealous of the attention he was getting, or if it was true, or what.

"How do you know that he scoops people?"

"He doesn't scoop everyone, he scoops young scientists that don't have a permanent position, yet. I know two grad students and three postdocs that say that he scooped their work."

He listened as Sam gave the details of each case which followed the same pattern: The young scientist would be visiting searching for their next postdoc or faculty position. They will have been invited to give a talk about their research. After the talk, Dr. Wolfschmidt would spend a lot of time with them going over the details of their research. Less than a month after their visit, Dr. Wolfschmidt would have reproduced their work as his and submitted it for publication before they had a chance.

"Even more cruel than stealing young people's research is that it is at a time in their lives when they are trying to build their careers, still in the process of becoming astrophysicists. For them every article is part of securing their future and Dr. Wolfschmidt steals that from them. It can be years of work that is flushed down the toilet," Sam explained.

"That is incredible."

Jeremy thought that five people saying it made a very strong case against Dr. Wolfschmidt; but, he still couldn't believe that he was getting away with doing it over and over again.

He questioned, "But, it isn't just the grad student or postdoc alone that he is stealing from...what about their advisors and collaborators? What about them? Don't they do something to stop him?"

"From what I've heard, it is nearly impossible to prove scooping or to do anything about it because it isn't a legal offense. It is similar to copyright and patents: if it isn't already published in some way, then it is first to publish or first to file is the winner."

"How about examining his computers? Everything we do has a creation date that is logged. It would be simple to show that Dr. Wolfschmidt had not been working on the topic before the scientist's visit..."

"You can't get access to his computers without permission or some kind of legal warrant. Every time he is accused, Dr. Wolfschmidt says that it was a project that he had started a long time ago but had put aside. He makes it sound as if he was the one

that was about to be scooped and thus he rushed to publish first!"

Jeremy's anger and frustration was not just for himself but for those many young scientists whose work had been stolen.

"I can't believe it."

"Yeah, I was really surprised to see him here at the Institute."

Without saying goodbye Jeremy rushed back to his lodging and got online. He thought about all the people in astrophysics that he trusted and who would be awake and who would know about Dr. Wolfschmidt. The perfect person was Franklin - he had been a graduate student in Dr. Wolfschmidt's department and he was an insomniac so worked almost all the time. Jeremy sent a quick note to Franklin asking about Dr. Wolfschmidt and scooping. Franklin answered by calling him.

"Jeremy, what's going on? Did you get scooped by Dr. Wolfschmidt?"

With those words, Jeremy knew that everything Sam had told him was the truth. All he could answer was, "Not yet..."

After explaining about the last twelve hours, Franklin had only one piece of advice: "You need to submit your article as soon as possible. Tonight if you can..."

Jeremy looked at the clock, it was already 11 pm. He was pretty sure that he could draft the paper quickly but he wouldn't be comfortable submitting it until he had a couple of days to proof read it.

"What if I put it on the astrophysics preprint server?"

"That isn't enough, you need to have submitted it to one of the journals. By the way, which part of your work is he stealing?"

"My method for identifying intermediate mass black holes."

"Wow, I didn't know that you were working on that problem. Astrophysicists have been searching for intermediate mass black holes for forty years. The only candidates were those found at the center for globular clusters, but since not every globular cluster had one, even that detection is shaky."

"Yeah, I know. The reason I hadn't published, yet,

is that I wanted to see if other scientists agreed that I was right. With my method, we are not searching for anything at optical wavelengths instead we see them in the UV, X-ray, and infrared, but they have to be visible in all three wavelength regions. Otherwise, there isn't enough flux for it to be an intermediate black hole."

"So, if you were observing in just one of those regions and found the object, you could misidentify it unless you checked the other two wavelengths?"

"That's it, essentially."

"That is definitely scoopable"

"Let me put on the coffee pot and get to work…"

"Yeah, you are going to have to…getting it submitted as soon as possible is the only way to be sure."

***

As Jeremy quickly redid his analysis, pulling together all the data he had collected, he thought to himself how had he been the last to know. Then he got angry again as he thought about why someone as unscrupulous as Dr. Wolfschmidt was included among the scientists at the Institute. Hours later, as he rewrote a sentence in his conclusions, he wondered how much of Dr. Wolfschmidt's reputation was built on stolen work. An hour after that, he finished formatting the article using LaTex as he pondered why Dr. Wolfschmidt went through the trouble of stealing other people's work when he was smart enough to do his own work. He thought that the man just saw the whole thing as a game in which he was clever enough to cheat and win. In a way, he had been repeatedly rewarded for cheating.

Jeremy submitted the article to the top journal in astrophysics knowing that it would get slammed by the reviewers because he was sure that there were errors that he couldn't see because he was so tired. Nonetheless, it was submitted by 5 am. Before going to sleep he sent a quick note to Sam and Franklin thanking them for the heads-up and letting them know that the article was submitted. He sleepily thought about what to say to Dr. Wolfschmidt when he saw him…

He slept most of the day, but was at the Institute for the afternoon talk which was about radio jets emanating from the center of distant galaxies. He noticed Dr. Wolfschmidt in the audience. He thought again about what he would say to him. Maybe he wouldn't even try to talk to him…

***

"Hello, Jeremy,"

Jeremy must have dozed off because people were filing out of the hall. He stretched and looked at the person that was speaking to him…Dr. Wolfschmidt.

He gave him a polite "Hello."

He was too tired to be more guarded.

Dr. Wolfschmidt smiled and said, "That was a good dinner last night. I was thinking about your verification process. Are you sure that it can be done only looking at UV, X-ray, and infrared observations?"

"Well, there is a wavelength dependence so you must look at the far UV and the longest X-ray wavelength you can. That way you sample enough to determine the peak that lies close to the transition. You are sampling both sides of the peak but not the maximum itself…"

Jeremy stopped speaking and wondered how had he gotten sucked into this conversation. Given what he knew about Wolfschmidt, like a fool he automatically answered any scientific question if he knew the answer. He inwardly slapped himself at his stupidity.

"That makes a lot of sense…I hope you get your article published soon."

"Yeah, it is already submitted. I'm waiting for the referee reports."

He watched a change come over Dr. Wolfschmidt's face.

Yup, that was shock, he thought to himself.

Jeremy felt victorious as he pivoted and left the hall walking into the cloud of white outside.

\#\#\#

Q. What is a Black Hole?

A. A black hole is a place in space where gravity pulls so much that even light can not get out. The gravity is so strong because matter has been squeezed into a tiny space. This can happen when a star is dying.

http://www.nasa.gov/audience/forstudents

EXTRA ES SOLAR
THE VISION

Dogearing Doris
by Moshe Prigan

Ralph Dimora came out of the bank and found a note under his car's windshield wiper.

"I'm at Shirley's Bar. Dean."

Ralph and Dean had been in and out of prison since childhood. Ralph always liked to hang around Dean and do him favors. He considered him smart, one who reads a lot of books. He walked across the street and entered the bar.

"I'm a member in a book readers club," Dean said and lit a cigar.

"I'm not surprised. You read tons of books in prison," Ralph said and drank from the black scotch.

"I want you to join me the club today," Dean said and took a deep puff. "One of the members, a lady named Doris, is doing things I hate." Dean said and twisted his lip.

"I would hate anybody who really gets on your nerves," Ralph said and lit a cigarette.

""The club meeting starts in about twenty minutes. Let's move."

They entered Dean's car and drove to the reading club.

"Listen. When we get there you don't fart a word. You just stay quiet from now on." Dean stared at him in the rear view mirror.

"I thought I would have to talk to Doris," Ralph said.

"You'll get your chance."

They approached a nice building facing a lake. They were six altogether. Molly, the facilitator, was a young diligent student of creative writing. There were Glen, a young priest, and Bill - a boxing trainer. And there was Doris, a big chested blonde.

Dean told the members that his friend was badly hit in his neck in a car accident and he wouldn't be able to talk until his vocal chords would be fully recovered.

"He's already read the book we've been discussing in the class," Dean said. Molly nodded in appreciation.

When she asked the group how the book had affected them and helped them to understand their relatives, or even themselves, Dean raised his hand.

"I reconciled the relationship with my father," he said. "He fell out with me more than ten years ago and we rarely met. The last part of this book softened my heart. I already went to see him."

Ralph surprised the group when he pulled a piece of folded paper out of his pocket and handed it to Doris who started reading:

"I had seen enough in Vietnam. After reading this book I had been involved in many of the anti-war efforts."

Doris noticed tears in Ralph's eyes and she moved her chair closer to him.

"Doris, do you like Stephen King?" Dean asked her during the break. "I have here his Dolores Claiborne."

"I loved it to pieces," she said. "She had a goddam life as I had with my goddam ex - husband. I would like to read it again."

"I would be more than glad to lend it to you," Dean said and opened his Samsonite slim case and took out the book.

"Oh My," Doris cried.

"Wait, you ain't seen nothing yet!" Dean said and opened it on the title page.

"It's signed. Stephen King autographed it for me."

"You're too kind, Dean." She was staring in his eyes. "It would be amazing as well as frightening to hold in my hands this book with Stephen King's signature."

"He wouldn't bite you." She exploded in a big laughter.

Ralph was sitting quietly, enjoying the salted crackers that Molly had put on the table.

"I'm a book lover, and when I read a book I take the dust jacket off."

"Sounds like stripping a woman off her dress," Doris said and grinned.

"Your literary imagination is impressive," Dean said.

"I think you're married to your books," She taunted him.

"I did love books more than my ex-wife who remarried a librarian," Dean said.

She took the book and thanked him.

\#

"Ralph, today is Christmas. Let's go see Doris," Dean said. "And don't forget the list."

"Yeah, the list," Ralph cheered.

They drove to Billington neighborhood. Ralph was holding a large bouquet and Dean brought Champagne.

"What a surprise," Doris cried.

"We missed you," Dean said.

"Same as me, guys."

She went to the kitchen and brought three elegant Champagne glasses on small saucers and a plate of snacks.

"Let's raise a toast, guys," Doris said.

They lifted their Champagne glasses, clinked them together in a toast and sipped. Then Dean opened a folded paper.

"Doris, I have here a list of things I personally hate that some members of the group have done during the meetings in the reading club."

"What things?" Doris said.

"Take Molly, for example," Dean said. "She, indeed, first took the dust jacket off her book but the spine was broken because she opened it too much while reading and she put the ashtray in the book to hold her place."

"Dean, you're obsessed with books," Doris said. Dean stood up and kept on preaching as if a talking machine had been planted in his head.

"Thickhead Bill never farted a word and he used the Hemingway book as a pillow whilst listening to Molly. I bet he stained the book with his stinking Brilliantine." He dropped back into his seat. Ralph was playing with his pocketknife.

"That was his book, not yours," Doris said.

"I saw you putting the cup of coffee on top of the book. No cleaning would erase the round stain you left on the book binding." He was staring at her.

"My book is not your business," she said. "You got derailed, Dean."

"I never leave a book open and face down to hold my place. It breaks the spine. Glen, the clumsy priest, did. Damn priest."

"But Dean, if you don't have a bookmark to keep your spot or your book doesn't have a ribbon – how would you find your last read page?" Doris tried to sooth him. "I, for one, put some piece of paper, like a receipt, or fold the corner of the page."

"Crap, I need to pee." He shuffled through to the bathroom.

He found his Dolores Claiborne on the toilet bowl tank. He came out holding his book.

"I found it on the toilet bowl tank," he said.

"So what?" Doris said.

"A signed copy is not meant to be read in toilet." Dean stifled the urge to scream. With a look of disgust he leafed through the book and found some folded corners. Then he opened to the title page.

"You dog-eared this page, Doris." Dean was trying hardly to conceal his rage.

"I did what?"

"Dooooooog-eared!" he yelled at her. "You folded down the top corner of the signed page. That's a crime."

Dean was almost on the verge of bursting into tears. He gave the book to Ralph.

"I am sorry, Dean. You shouldn't have lent me a book that you refer to as the dearest thing in the world."

Doris stood up to take the glasses to the kitchen. Dean pointed with his finger to his lips and winked at Ralph.

"You committed a crime, Doris."

The voice behind her back sounded unfamiliar to her. She turned her face and got a shock when she saw Ralph. He hit her head several times with the sharp corners of the book. She let out a hoarse scream and fell down on the floor, facing the carpet. Then Ralph took out from the inside of his coat a big nickel staple gun. It read: FOR HEAVY DUTY. He folded her left upper ear, pressed it hard to her left temple and shot three times. She was moaning.

Then Ralph pulled up her dressing gown above

her hips and pulled down her white panties. He pulled out a black marker. On the left bum cheek Ralph wrote: have respect, and on her right one he wrote: for signed books.

"Let's get the hell outta here," Dean said.

They left the house.

Fastening his seat belt in Dean's car, Ralph said: "Dean, the book we left there was still good for reading."

"Blood stained. It will distract the reader." He started the engine.

"It must be worth something," Ralph didn't let.

"Signature was a fake, and you heavily bumped the corners." His voice sounded somewhat broken to Ralph.

"One day soon I'll get another one for you," said Ralph, trying to cheer him up.

They followed the night.

END

The International Flag of Planet Earth

Tachyon Node
All Fiction
Not Just
Science Fiction

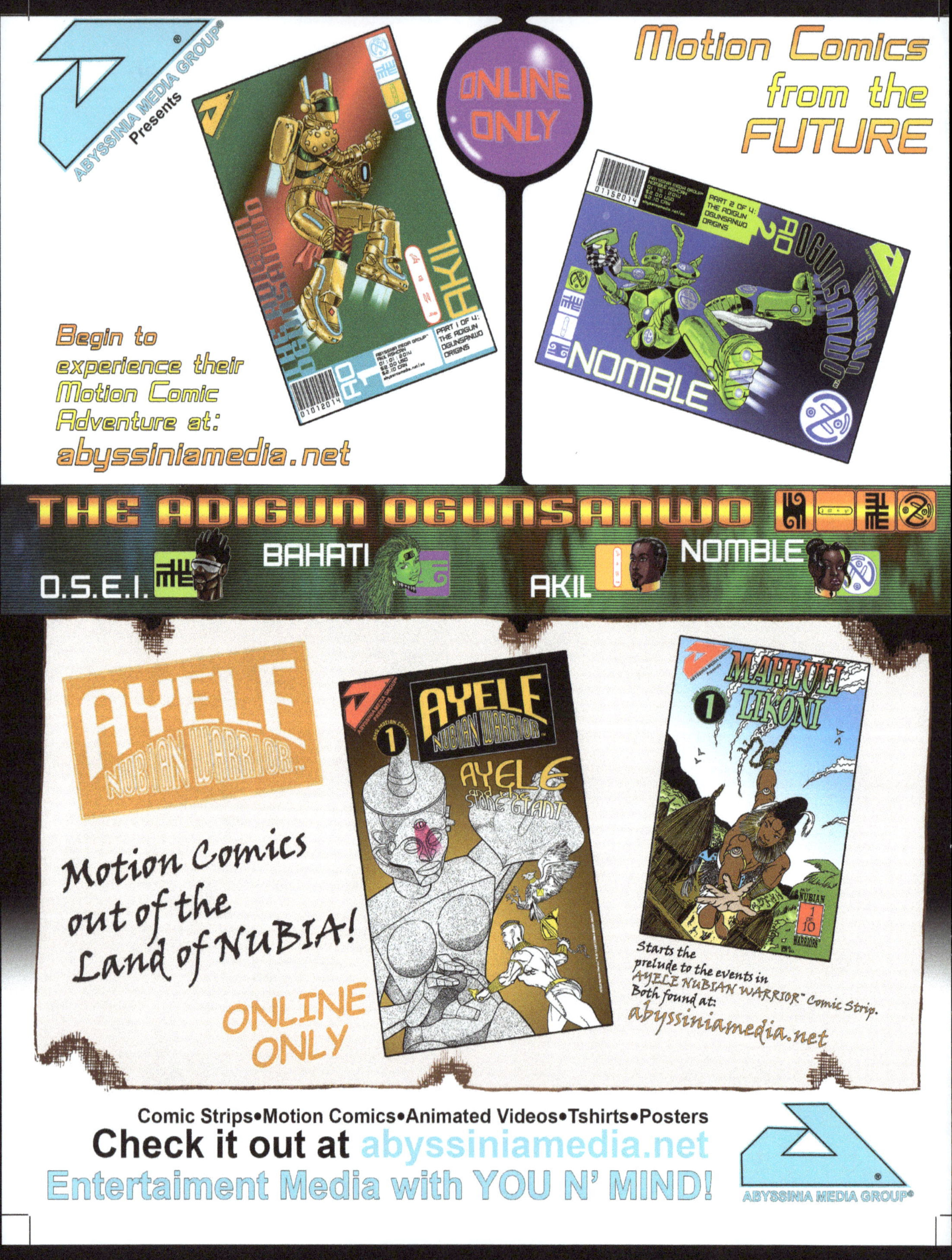

Thanatos

NDESTINITY

THE TEMPLE
EXTRASOLAR

J. Ryan Malone 2011

Maelstrom
EXTRA S SOLAR

Barren Rim   EXTRASSOLAR

CARHAYAKEN RING
OUR LAST CHANCE - ONE EARTH - BILLIONS OF HUMANS

EXTRA SOLAR
HUNTERS

GUARDIANPRIME
GENESIS

WWW.THECOMICREPUBLIC.COM

Do Not Wake The Beast

Part 1

By Patricia I. Williams

The tavern door opened, then smacked against the wall so hard the timbers shivered and creaked. The startled inhabitants could only gap as the storm rushed in chilling their already wet bodies. Sleet and icy rain swirled through doorway and spat upon the patrons relegated to the dirt floor near it. Some grumbled and scuttled away from the muddy puddles as ice and rain pelted the interior. The barkeep rushed to close the door only to shriek when a dark shadow detached itself from the storm, moving into the common room.

The shaggy apparition moved the frightened man aside by stepping into his space. The door swung back and closed with another bang. The bar dropped across it, leaving the bitter weather to slap and push from the outside. A rough cloak dropped from a set of massive shoulders. The collective sighed with relief at the tall male figure. Oh, well not a demon, just another mercenary.

Raven hung his dripping cloak on the hook near the door and rung the water from the dark braid draped around his neck. He already knew how many men sat at the greasy tables and that any women here had long since gone to bed in the cramped musty upper rooms. He turned on the still stupefied bartender.

"Boil some water, now."

"Water, boil water?"

"Water, now."

Raven crossed the dark room, removing the sword hanging from his back to a table nearest the soot darkened back wall. He pulled the table away and settled in the rickety chair that groaned under his weight. He ignored the bleary eyes peering at him and the stench of wet unwashed bodies. He took a leather pouch from the thick belt he wore and placed it on the table along with his damp travel bag. The

barkeep rushed to the table holding a battered kettle, the handle wrapped by the bottom of his dirty apron.

"A tankard and the kettle before the water's cold." Raven growled at the seemingly witless man.

"Oh, yes, a tankard. Yes...yes sir...I yes." He scurried away again the kettle swinging wildly, causing swearing occupants of the floor and tables to duck and move from his path. Raven glared. The man finally stumbled back, dropping the tankard so it rolled across the table. The warrior's hand closed around it. The kettle banged against the side of the table, splashing water on the hapless bartender. He managed to put the kettle down and back away. One more glance from the warrior at the table sent him back to his duties on trembling legs.

Raven poured a portion of dried herbs into the tankard and filled it with water. He warmed his cold hands in the steam from the cup. After a few minutes he raised it to his lips. The first sip nearly forced a groan from the exhausted man. He had to really control the urge to gulp the bitter liquid down and scald his throat. The heat settled in his belly, warming him completely after a while. He finally relaxed against the wall and let his eyes travel openly around the room. Most of the inhabitants avoided his gaze.

There were just as many brigands as honest travelers in the room. His size and the gleaming steel of his sword should prevent any one from getting ideas about lifting his purse. He chuckled out loud at the thought because his purse was painfully thin right now. He was hoarding what remained in anticipation of a new job, hence the smelly hovel having to do for for this moment. He rested his head on the wall to doze, at least content the tavern was shielded by a hill that blocked the winds from blowing through the ill fitted logs at his back. He did not move as the people in the room finally settled once more before the meager fire.

The strong slept near the flames, the not so bold lay shivering in the cold and enduring the draft whistling through the ramshackle walls and around the ill fitted door. After a while, Raven pulled a woolen blanket from his pack and wrapped it around himself. He allowed himself to relax, just a little, in the heavy folds and went to sleep.

Silence awakened him. The storm was over for now. He folded the blanket tightly and stuffed it into his pack. He knew the sun had risen, although he expected the day would be sullen with clouds, fog and more rain. The slide of metal on leather stirred some of the other wayfarers. Grabbing his still damp cloak, Raven stepped across bodies on the floor and lifted the bar from the door. He slipped into the chilly morning, crossing quickly to the shed to fetch his horses. The animals were nosing around in ice-rimmed hay. He slipped a bag of oats over their noses and rubbed them down before tossing blanket and saddle on his mount. Very soon, the animal would refuse the grains and need to hunt or Raven would have to buy fresh meat. He reloaded all his gear on the shaggy packhorse and stepped into the saddle.

Chi walked carefully, wary of the cracking ice and mud sliding beneath his hooves. Raven looked around at the dull winter landscape and figured he had at least a six-hour ride to the next tavern along the twisting, treacherous track passing for a road. He hoped to make it before the weather soured again. Another night in a filthy roadside tavern would not improve his mood. Sighing heavily he guided his animals off into the tall pines, growling as wind blown water cascaded down from the trees. The rumble of distant thunder herald another round of storms.

The mercenary had heard a local lord, new to his position, was hiring men-at-arms to shore up his troops. Fighters from all over the Midlands were finding their way to these sparsely populated mountains. NorBlad raiders would be scouring the land very soon. It was said the old master of the lands paid tribute to the northern fighters but the peasants and lesser nobles still lost too much to the raiders.

There should be fighting aplenty and gold for his war bag.

From time to time he dozed in the saddle aware that Chi would let him know if trouble approached.

Like him, the animal stood out in this land of dark pine forest and snow. Iron gray with black stockings, mane and tail, his muzzle and face were black as well. Chi hailed from the far western plains. The animal enabled the mercenary to charge twice the fees offered for only his sword. More than once Raven had literally been plucked from death's jaws by his oft times vicious guardian. Chi was heavily boned and muscled with deceptively gentle dark eyes. His teeth were dagger long and sharp edged, dealing deep and grievous wounds. Tales were told that they were not true horses, but demon spawn erupting on the western plains during a fight between the gods. Raven always wondered if there was more truth than not to the tale. The demons chose their riders and seemed to anticipate their needs. They also had a sack of gall in their throats, which injected into a bite caused a lingering agonizing death. No one else rode him, no one dared. Savage, the animals were known to kill other four legs for food including their own kind.

*****

Torches were just being lit within the timber walled city of Virgilia when Raven finally reached the gate days later. The guardsmen paid little attention to Chi. In the dark he appeared just like any other horse and Raven was grateful. He had no wish to spend the evening in the cold arguing with superstitious men. Once inside he realized the city was teeming with people.

Observation determined many of the farmers from the countryside had moved into the city. Resigned to a longer wait for bed and a meal, Raven traveled through the town until arriving on the paths just below the high road to the lord's residence. Taverns, choked with smoke and rank odors, rang with off key music and fighting. The upper paths hosted the higher priced inns for the more sedate clientele. There would be people from the richer farms, merchants and nobles. Raven listened to the chatter from the throng pushing and shoving along the narrow torch lit way. Though disconcerted at finding a horse barring their way, most of the people were too inebriated to do more than stumble from his path. Hawkers stood in front of the doors, shouting about the best wines, feather mattresses and of course who had the fattest and cleanest bed warmers. He pondered over the gold left in his purse and finally decided to move a little closer to his goal. The best place would have a large barn where Chi could rest away from the majority of animals. Oddly, though he was a stallion, the animal did not insight other horses to fight, but they were very nervous around him.

He came to a place with a gate and a wall nearly his height surrounding it. Lamps and a bell hung from the posts. Further along the wall he could see an even wider gate, probably for carriages and wagons to come and go. Faint music could be heard over the rabble in the road. Decision made, he rang the bell.

After a time, a small head popped up under the bell.

"An ya bizna bein'?"

"What else would I be here for? Open the gate brat!"

"Tha li ya havin' na coin!" The guardian of the gate assessed Raven with an exaggerated leer only to have a hand surround his head and lift him from his perch.

"Open the damn gate, or I will open it with your head." Raven growled, squeezing the bug-eyed boy's skull. Torchlight reflected in the catlike eyes of the monster crushing his head. Frightened spitless, the youngster scrabbled at the wooden bar, arms and legs flailing wildly. He managed to lift it just enough that Raven dropped him and grabbed the heavy log. It was little effort to toss the bar over the head of the boy. He flinched as it hit the ground, one end narrowly missing his head. Chi pushed through the gate and the boy scrambled from his path.

"You don't decide for a man where his coin is spent brat. Keepers of gates can be slaves on the morrow."

The gulp was audible as the boy scrambled to his feet and hurried to get the bar back up on the gate. He would endure the dampness of his ragged britches for the remainder of his shift, but have two fights later on unable to endure the taunting about his smelly condition.

Raven rode across the yard and stepped down before the main doors of a very large inn. To one side he could see a taproom filled with revelers. Well to do nobles and merchants communed together. Tomorrow in his lordships residence they would pretend ignorance of each other. He stepped through double doors. The main lobby was well lit and he was not surprised to see a very fat tavern keeper leaning against a podium. This one obviously trusted no one to collect his coin. How else could he maintain the mountain of flesh that covered his slim bones? Raven stepped up to the counter. Before the man could launch into his tirade the mercenary dropped a very small bag on the ledger book.

"See here now..."

"Look in the pouch before you give me any sass, old man."

Insulted, the man just prevented himself from calling for his bouncers. He untied the drawstring and poured two gold coins into this palm. Instantly his expression changed, to suspicion.

"I'm no thief, you greedy bastard. Say I am and taste steel."

"I, I would not dream of it. No sir, did...did not, er...cross my mind."

Raven scowled at the innkeeper. The man visibly shrank under the pale silver gaze of the mercenary.

"How many nights will that buy me and care for my horses?"

The coins disappeared into the chubby hands, then the man sank his teeth into the coin. On further inspection a smile creased his face until his eyes disappeared. His bite left marks in the soft metal.

"Forgive me sir, a man cannot be too careful in these trying times. Come, come this way. Why I will escort you myself. Yes yes, this will afford you one of our best rooms and food for at least a moon."

"My animals need tending and my bags brought in."

"I have ser..."

"I tend my own things."

"As you wish...of course. Right this way."

Raven followed the man up two flights of stairs and a turn to the left. The room was larger than expected and the bed even larger. Servants scurried in behind him, rushing to light the kindling in the fireplace and turn back the covers. The innkeeper lit the candles in the scones near the door. A pitcher of water and a basin were brought in. He checked the bed, pleasantly surprised to find it feathered and not filled with straw. The covers were soft wool and it even had pillows. There were no connecting doors and the one window looked out over the rear yard. That pleased him. The barn was directly across from his room.

"This will do innkeeper. Bring whatever you have left in your kitchen this hour for a hungry man. I do not expect a full meal this late. Listen closely to what I tell you. I do not require wine or ale. A good strong tea is all right, if you have it. If not, keep hot water on boil for me. I have my own herbs and I drink at odd times. I like my food cooked plain. Leave the fancy sauces for those in your taproom. A tub of hot water now, I would be rid of the trail dust. Tell your stable hands that my packhorse may be cared for, but my stallion is not to be touched. Curiosity will get them killed and I will not pay gold to the family of a stupid child. We understand each other innkeeper?"

"Perfectly, absolutely sir. I will give the orders at once. Come along everyone. There is much to get done, and other quest to see too. Come along, come along. Oh sir, my name is Milty. Call on me whatever you need."

He bowed and moved his sweaty bulk from the room. Raven opened the window wide to air the room before going down the stairs to tend Chi and the packhorse.

Raven walked the animals around the building to the barn. The innkeeper was already there yelling at the stable boys about his horse. All eyes bugged as they got a close look at the prancing war stallion. The mercenary growled softly into one pricked ear.

"Stop making a spectacle of yourself, you conceited ass. I do not need to peel some stupid boy off the bottom of your horseshoe in the morning."

Chi snorted and arched his neck, stepping higher, tail waving like a banner behind him. Suddenly his long neck snaked out and those talon sharp teeth snapped together. Everyone jumped in shock.

"You have been warned. He is trained for the battlefield. Don't go near him."

With that Raven led his animals into the barn. He unloaded the pack animal and gave him over to one of the stable hands. Then he went to the back of the barn, guiding Chi into an empty stall. Chi nibbled at Raven's hair and pulled on his leather shirt during the removal of his saddle and the necessary rubdown. The mercenary ignored him, too tired to appreciate the animal's joy at being out of the cold rainy weather. He did chuckle, however, when Chi's ears lay flat discovering his trough was to be filled with fresh oats instead of meat.

"I will feed you in the morning horse. I am too tired to deal with a nosy landlord this night." He was pushed into the side of the stall for his negligence and so removed himself rather quickly.

"Don't take your bad mood out on anyone I must bury in the morning Chi."

He noted the stable hands watching with some trepidation and knew he would sleep without worry. Raven hung his weapon's bag across his shoulders, picked up his travel bags and hauled the awkward load through the back door of the inn. As he suspected there were stairs to the left and right leading to the upper floors. Servants ran up and down, in and out of the kitchen, shifting around him like fish in a pond. The last of the servants were struggling up the two flights with buckets of water, possibly for for him. Raven shivered at the thought of settling into hot soapy water. He walked in and put his bags on the bed.

On a low table near the fireplace was a cloth-covered tray. A kettle sat on a metal plate near the fire, steam rising from the spout. A chair with a high back had been placed before the flames. The warrior smiled to think of the landlord snatching it from the first floor rooms to grace a land less mercenary's dwelling. Raven was glad he hoarded the last fee. He could present himself well rested and there were enough silvers left to buy him new shirts and possibly new boots. A prosperous appearance would impress the uninitiated before tales of battles won.

The last of the servants bowed out of the room, so Raven barred the door. He stripped down and put his sweaty leathers and smelly cloak in the bag for that purpose. In the morning the cloak would be washed and he would clean and oil his leathers. From one pouch Raven sprinkled crushed green leaves over the steaming bath water. After a time the smell of eucalyptus filled the room. Breathing deeply, the herbs eased the tightness in his chest. Illness dare not take hold when a job was at stake. He put a chunk of hard milled soap and a clean rag on the floor by the tub. Then filled his tankard with herbs from another pouch and poured the hot water over them leaving it to steep.

The platter on the table had thick slices of warm bread spread with, from the smell of it, goat cheese and a bowl of venison stew. He sat down immediately to eat, wiping up the last of the gravy with the bread. Drank the hot tea and finally relaxed.

Raven lowered his body into the tub and sighed with relief. Too tired to soak without falling asleep, he washed his hair and soaped the grime of his journey away. He rinsed with the two buckets left next to the tub and dried off with the bath sheets left by the servants. For a fighter, used to bathing in cold streams, this was luxury indeed.

Hair drying and braided once more, Raven stowed his gear under the bed, except for a short sword that looked like a big dagger in his large hands. It would lie next to him in bed. He blew out the candles, leaving his window partially open and the curtains pulled back. Satisfied with his precautions, Raven crawled into bed and sank gratefully into plump pillows and clean bedding.

Light filled the room before he woke. He pulled the bar from the door and went about the business of dressing for the day. Almost immediately the door opened and men began to empty the tub of the dirty water. Once empty they would take the tub down and wash it out. He congratulated himself once again that frugality was such a part of his life. Too many of his ilk drank and whored all their earnings away. They would not be eating well or present themselves clean and correctly attired.

He paid but scant attention to the servants once he was aware they posed no threat to him. But they were taking in as much as they could for gossip later. The tavern girls would love to know more about the big warrior that had pushed his way into Milty's Tavern and Beds. Like most they had known, his muscled body was covered with scars. One vicious burn marked his back from shoulder to buttocks. When he turned to watch another arrival deliver his breakfast, they noted he was not small in the place that mattered to wenches, but a ring of what appeared to be gold pierced it and his nipples!

Raven cradled his staff and balls into an odd quilted pouch and secured it by thin leather straps across his hips. He sat on the bed to pull on heavy stockings, wool breeches and boots. The tub was dragged from the room as he sat down to eat.

The landlord could be commended. He knew how to feed a hungry man. A half loaf of bread, a pot each of butter and honey, and hot porridge laced with nuts had been delivered. A metal platter held thick slices of ham, four boiled eggs and a serving of wild greens. He ate heartily washing it all down with another tankard of tea.

He finished dressing, putting on a thick wool shirt, his hunting knife and buckskin coat. He sat the tray outside the door and walked down the back stairs to the kitchen. Waving the cook over, he asked the woman if it was possible to purchase any fresh meat in town. She told him hunters came to the market during the winter. They went out everyday now because so many people had come to town. She gave him directions and he thanked her and went to the barn.

Chi stood with his head hanging over the stall door staring in Raven's direction. His black lips were drawn back, odd white fangs exposed and glistening with saliva drooling onto the floor. The hair on the mercenary's body stood up. He could only stare back. It took more than a moment to shake off the instinctive fear that gripped him. Chi could still scare him and he hated that fact.

"Stop glaring at me you devil. If my life is so bad, go back to the plains."

He physically shook off the shiver that raced down his spine.

"All right, I said I would get meat this morning and I will."

Chi jerked his head back, and then trotted the length of the barn. He butted Raven gently, nuzzling his neck chest and belly. Chi was, maybe, a little contrite. Raven shook his head, caressed the soft muzzle and scratched behind the horse's ears. Chi's forked tongue slipped around his wrists and flickered about catching his scent. The mercenary stepped closer and wrapped his arms around Chi's neck. For a time they communed together in silence, the horse supporting his weight.

Raven did not understand the connection. He sometimes wondered if he felt anything at all. But for an undetermined moment he was just not "here" when horse and rider made good morning. He would have gladly avoided this morning's appraisal, however. As surely has the sun came up Chi would never hurt him, but then Chi was and was not what he appeared. Like a well-trained warrior, the horse kept him on alert. Life had taught Raven much, a friend today could be stabbing you tomorrow. What ability to trust remained to the man centered on his steed. Chi instructed him as well as protected.

"Come along. The cook says there is a market off the high road. If the meat is not fresh kill we will go hunting together."

Chi danced away, impatient to get moving. Raven left by the wagon gate, propped open to allow vendors to bring in fresh supplies. The horse paced him, eyes surveying his surroundings. Cooks and helpers were coming and going, some with wagons of fresh goods for the inns and taverns. Raven picked up his pace. He ducked into a side road and followed it until he came to a field separated from the buildings by a low wall. It was nothing to hop over. The hunters were here, sharing the wide grassy lot with the tents of itinerant merchants and a few farmers. Chi would choose and Raven would buy whatever he wanted.

The hunters were cleaning the site after a morning of butchering. They were surprised by the big man and horse appearing among them. Quickly enough they realized he was actually there to buy. Chi sniffed and nudged deer, mountain goat and even bear. His actions garnered more than a few comments. Raven was beginning to think they would have to hunt themselves, when another hunter rode in, animals still strapped to his pack horses. Some of the men heckled him for his late arrival. Chi immediately turned to follow him. The hunter looked over his shoulder at the pair and scowled. He stepped from the saddle and turned ready to fight if need be.

"Wha ya want. I ha wor ta da."

Raven frowned in return and growled.

"I came to buy meat. What else would I be doing here?"

"Humph. It loo lake na merchant."

"What I am is no concern of yours. I have silver. You are late and money has already been missed. Do I buy or take my money someplace else?"

"Na dress ye. Ha ta wa."

Raven looked to Chi. The horse was tugging at one of the carcasses.

"How much for that buck, now."

"I ga gol fa buck."

Raven laughed.

"By the time any cooks come back your meat will not be worth ten coppers. Sell me the buck. Two silvers and you don't even have to dress it."

"Sa silva loo silva."

Raven slipped the silver coins from his pouch and tossed them in the air. A dirty bloodied hand caught them. He turned away to help Chi pull off the carcass.

"Whoa tha. I ga it, sta has slabber on evathi!"

Raven stopped the man's advance with a big hand smacked against his chest.

"I will cut it down. You stay away from my horse."

The man wanted to complain further, but the irritated squint from those hard eyes stopped him cold. He watched closely, however, making sure they did not take what was not paid for. Raven cut the rawhide tying the legs together and heaved the carcass over Chi's back.

"Go beast and eat in private. I have clothes to buy."

The horse snorted and walked away from the

hunters toward a distant stand of trees. Raven rarely watched Chi consume his kills. It was enough to see what he did to enemies in battle. After a meal there was no more than skin, skull and hipbones left. Pretty much all activity stopped when the men realized the horse was leaving and Raven was walking back to the center of the market.

Signs to ward off evil fluttered from one hand to another. Speculation would be all over town by the time torches were lit for the night. A Thanatu warrior and his stallion had come to Virgilia.

End of Part 1

Beneath Red Tail Wings
Patricia I. Williams
Available Online at all major bookstores

Q.A.A.S
(Questions Answered About Science)

This graphic, on the right, depicts paths by which carbon has been exchanged between Martian interior, surface rocks, polar caps, waters and atmosphere, and also depicts a mechanism by which carbon is lost from the atmosphere with a strong effect on isotope ratio.

Carbon dioxide (CO2) to generate the Martian atmosphere originated in the planet's mantle and has been released directly through volcanoes or trapped in rocks crystallized from magmas and released later. Once in the atmosphere, the CO2 can exchange with the polar caps, passing from gas to ice and back to gas again. The CO2 can also dissolve into waters, which can then precipitate out solid carbonates, either in lakes at the surface or in shallow aquifers.

Carbon dioxide gas in the atmosphere is continually lost to space at a rate controlled in part by the sun's activity. One loss mechanism is called ultraviolet photodissociation. It occurs when ultraviolet radiation (indicated on the graphic as "hv") encounters a CO2 molecule, breaking the bonds to first form carbon monoxide (CO) molecules and then carbon (C) atoms. The ratio of carbon isotopes remaining in the atmosphere is affected as these carbon atoms are lost to space, because the lighter carbon-12 (12C) isotope is more easily removed than the heavier carbon-13 (13C) isotope. This fractionation, the preferential loss of carbon-12 to space, leaves a fingerprint: enrichment of the heavy carbon-13 isotope, measured in the atmosphere of Mars today.

Image Credit:
Lance Hayashida/Caltech
Last Updated: Nov. 24, 2015
Editor: Tony Greicius

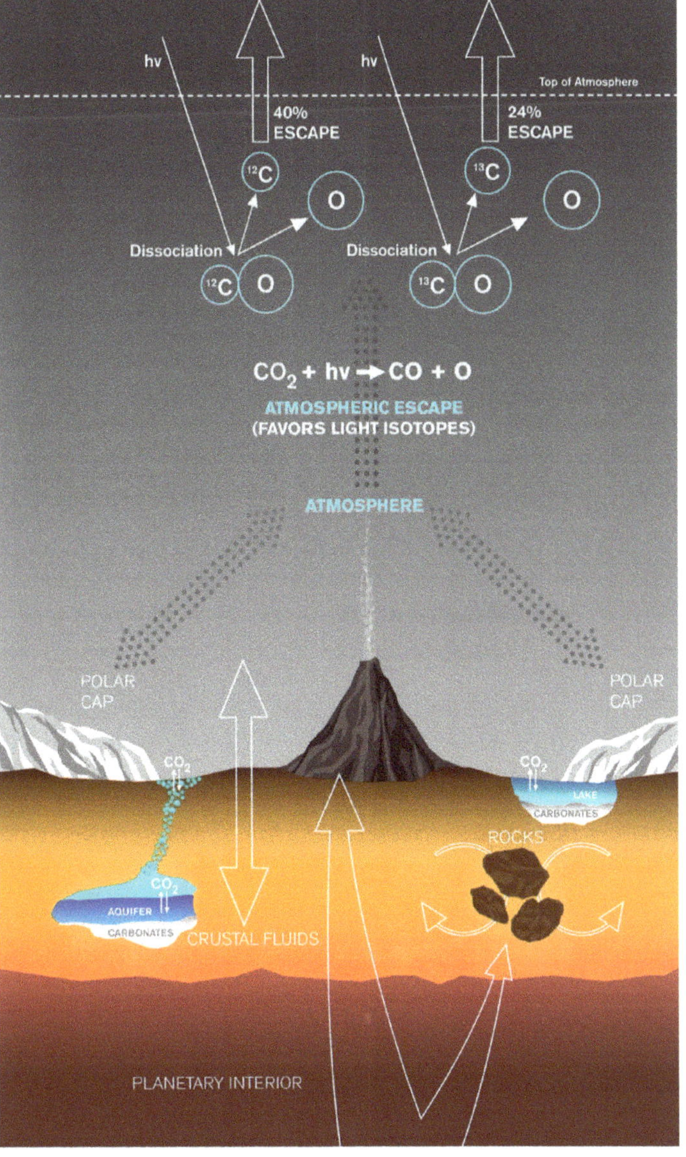

Mythical Legends Publishing

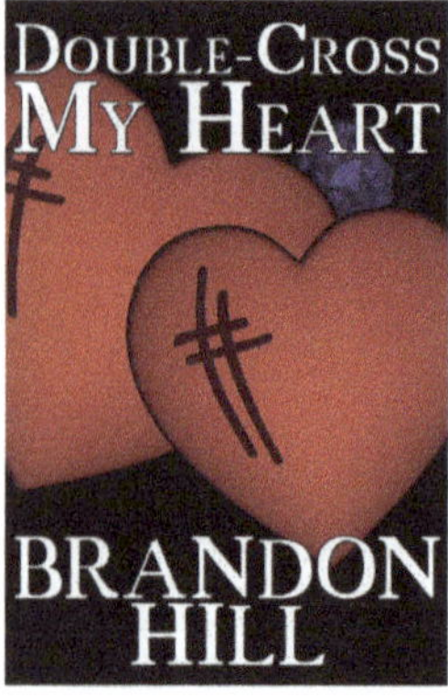

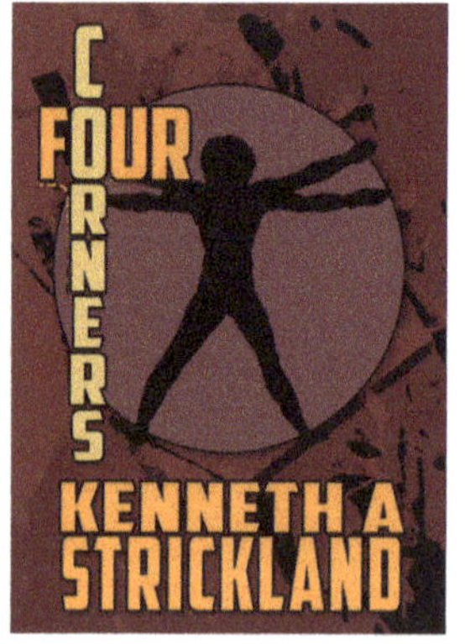

WE BUILD DREAMS

http://mythicallegends.com

The Missing Heart

by Kenneth A. Strickland

It was one of those hot southern days, the kind that made you want to crawl into an ice filled bath and stay there.

Marlon Stevedore had seen a lot of those days, and he wanted to see more. He'd done well in his life and now that life was threatened. His heart was failing him and he wanted to keep on living. 63 years was not enough as far as he was concerned. And it wasn't fair, he'd earned a great fulfilling life and made a lot of money.

Now that money was to become worthless.

All the struggle, all the brilliance was about to go poof.

He lay in his bed and watched the news of freaks on TV. The people of Four Corners. They had double everything, and here his heart was failing him as he needed it most.

Marlon Stevedore watched as they went about their business and lived their lives and his was fading and they didn't care, why should they? He wasn't one of them.

But they had two hearts. They could live on one and be none the worse for it. He could make a good offer, practically anything they wanted. All any of them needed to do was give him one. If they didn't accept the offer, he would take one, pay the donor and apologize later. After all, it wouldn't hurt for them to give a dying man their extra heart.

Stevedore made sure the facilities for taking the heart were in place in his mansion. He made sure that the state of the art transplant operations room was ready in one of the back houses. The place was made sanitary and clean, a virtual clean room that had filtration systems and purified water for the surgeons to clean themselves. There would be no chances taken with this operation.

The mutants of Four Corners were fascinating everyone, and doctors speculated that they could live without an organ if it were removed. If they did this right, the mutant would be opened and their questions might well be answered and he would get a new heart. Stevedore couldn't wait. He'd made the offer for one of their hearts, and he'd been rebuffed. The mutants rejected the offer as if they smelled something bad and wanted no part of it.

Well, he supposed, what did he expect? After all the mutants lived without telling anyone they were there and they must have liked their privacy. Well that was over, Stevedore thought. They had no right to be so selfish when there was a greater need than one solitary, single mutant life when an important man needed what they had.

Still, his people had to kidnap, and he hated that word, a mutant, do the operation and get the heart. Very simple. They watched the local college for mutants and found a candidate. Most of the young men from Four Corners was strapping, and strong. As his secretary put it, built like a brickhouse.

Stevedore laughed when he heard that. It was a dry chuckle really since he couldn't give a big roaring laugh like he used to. He had to put the oxygen mask on because he wanted to laugh and it hurt too much.

His nurse came into the room and adjusted the mask on him as he coughed with a racking spasm. It was a long time before he calmed down and he tried to breath carefully and regain his composure.

In came his aide, Kermit Walden in his bowtie and bush cut and glasses. He stepped carefully to the man and asked, all you all right, Mr. Stevedore?"

Stevedore looked at him through rheumy "I will be if you've done what you've supposed to do, yes."

"We have located the donor and are making the pickup tomorrow. It shouldn't be a problem." Walden said.

"Make sure there isn't a problem, Walden. Make sure we have all the particulars about this young man and be ready to transfer the money when the operation is done." Stevedore said. "We will owe him that at least."

"Yes sir." Walden said and went to make the arrangements.

It was two weeks before Henry Dozier woke up with IV in his arms and a new scar on his chest.

Weakly, he pushed aside the robe and saw the scar and began to weep. He screamed his horror and then a doctor came into the room and looked him over. His heart was steady, the doctor thought, and they did a good job making sure that all the plumbing worked. What was the fury about?

"Look, you're all right," the doctor said. "We made sure to keep your heart together so that it could do its job…"

Henry looked at him with a cold fury. "You arrogant ass! We can't survive for long with only one heart. Our hearts work in tandem you fool! There's going to be too much stress on one heart!"

"All our preliminary studies say you can live on one heart…" Doctor Frank Waller said.

"Your preliminary studies? Where did you do them, In a sandbox?" asked Henry. "You've killed me! You know nothing about us and you've killed me! That crazy old man killed me!"

Henry turned his face away from Waller and sobbed. Waller knew that Stevedore made the offer to Four Corners openly. The reaction was expected, Waller thought, but not this. If what Dozier said was true, then they might have committed murder trying to save one elderly man.

Back in Four Corners, the news that Henry Dozier going missing was news, and Sheriff Jim Mosley had his suspicions, so did the rest of the town. If the old man took young Henry, that mean they might have done the operation and taken one of the hearts. Henry couldn't survive for long with a missing heart. He might have two months if he were lucky.

They checked Henry's college roommates. It would make sense if they saw who took Henry, but Mosley knew it was possible that none saw the kidnapping. They had to find Henry and soon.

"Sheriff?" Karla Morgan came into the office where Jim Mosley was standing in front of map of the area.

Mosley turned to her. "What have you got?"

"There are reports that there was a caravan of cars driving up to the Stevedore mansion within four weeks ago. That fits in with the time that Henry went missing. There are also reports of medical supplies being delivered to the Stevedore mansion about a year before that. We did these…" Karla showed him a set of surveillance photos of the mansion. She pointed to the back house. There was a circle around a white robed man and woman leaving the house.

"That has to be where he is." Mosley said with a hint of disgust. "We have to scramble a medical team and get over there. We might be in time to save two lives."

The caravan drove up to the Stevedore mansion and when the guard at the gate refused to let them in, they drove through the gate. They didn't feel a need to be polite.

Dr. Jeff Murdock got out and when the guard confronted him with a weapon, Murdock and his guard pulled out submachine guns ready to fire. The others in the caravan jumped out and pointed guns at the men trying to stop them.

"Let's stop this nonsense and get me to the so called doctor that did the operation that took the heart from our mutant brother." Murdock said. "We know he is here."

"You can save both their lives?" asked Walden looking at the big fifty foot medical van.

"That's what we're here for." Murdock said.

Both men were examined. The doctors that did the operation was shown why it couldn't work. Both men were put on life support and the stolen heart was examined and found to be worthless. It was failing slowly and Stevedore's condition was getting worse.

"Look, all our research said he should be able to live with just the one heart." Dr, Frank Waller said defensively.

Dr. Jeff Murdock kept his eyes on his work. Making sure the nerves were connected was more important than screaming at him. "I am willing to tell you how to do your job. You've just found out about us and what we have in our bodies, and not much at that. We are not a surplus parts store where you can just go and pick up something for the kids, alright?"

"We made an honest offer for one heart? Why is this so important?" Waller asked.

Murdock looked at him with disgust. "The Hippocratic oath says, first do no harm. If you can't see you have done harm, them constantly killing us as you take our hearts while your patient gets worse or dies is not helping."

Waller could feel the contempt Murdock had for him and the obvious repulsion at his actions.

"If you cannot learn that you have made a major mistake and both men are in deep kimchee right now, then God help you and anyone that comes to you for help."

The cloning techniques were used to grow two new hearts and after three days, installed in the patients.

Murdock carefully stitched the new heart in carefully, and started it up. Both doctors watched as it started up and Waller felt a load off of his mind as both men were wheeled into the recovery area and stabilized before they were taken back into the house.

The doctors were given the strictest warning that if they ever tried it again, even their families' lives would be forfeit. They were also given a three volume set of "Human Cloning and Their Practical Possibilities" by Four Corners Press.

Two months later a limousine drove up to Henry Dozier's house where he was playing with his German Shepherd, Skye. The dog fetched the thrown ball just as Marlon Stevedore stepped out the car. The lawyers from Four Corners met with Stevedore's lawyers and hashed out a settlement that made Henry very rich and kept Stevedore from going through a potentially embarrassing trial, and giving others the same idea.

Marlon Stevedore walked to Henry Dozier and stopped. The tension was thick and Henry had no interest seeing or speaking to the man. He did look like recovered somewhat and he had good color and seemed to be strong.

"I had to come by and see how you were." Stevedore said.

Henry said nothing.

"I suppose I'm the last person you want to see after all of this. I don't blame you. But I wanted to live. I thought you would too, even after we took your heart. I'm sorry." Stevedore stood and waited for the flood of curses and or the blow he thought Henry would give him.

Henry spat on the grass between them. "I will never forgive you for thinking the world couldn't do without you, or your arrogance in taking my heart. Don't let the door it you in the ass, and don't let me see you again."

Marlon Stevedore wanted to restate his apology, but he knew it was a worthless act. He turned on his heel, got in his car and drove away.

Henry watched with contempt as the limo disappeared around a corner.

Forgiveness is never easy.

###

Four Corners
by Kenneth A. Strickland
Available in all bookstores and online

CHRISTINE TAYLOR-BUTLER
Sacred Mountain
EVEREST
Explorers
The Nervous System

STAR TREK: The Modern Myth

by Tachyon Node Staff

Some time ago I attended a session, sponsored by a local church, called The Spirit of Star Trek. During this session, one of the speakers likened Star Trek as the modern myth. Let that sink in for a few seconds - The modern myth. He went on the say that Star Trek is probably the only franchise in the history of the world that has no boundaries or divisible lines. It is the ultimate humanist. Trek exists "by which truth and morality is sought through human investigation." Each generation of Trek dealt with the human suffrage of the time. As Humans inched our way through the stream of time we changed. Our morals changed with new knowledge of the self and information fueled the fire for further discovering of the self.

This is where Trek finds its stride and runs for the long haul. Its recent orgiastic leap has taken humans across a field of dreams in which anything is possible and all things have a solution. Trek has become our vehicle for telling the story of humankind. With our marbles intact and our wits tethered to the ball of sanity we spin a yarn of truths, half-truths, and never-truths. Trek is the modern myth.

A myth by definition is typically an ancient story dealing with supernatural beings, ancestors, heroes, and the gods. It purports to explain natural occurrences and cultural practices, both ethically and morally. The story of Prometheus is about humankind acquiring fire and the emergence of sacrifices. It's about the differences between mortals and immortals and our willingness to defy the gods even in the face of eminent discomfort or death.

"Where No Man Has Gone Before," places our hero Kirk against a new god Mitchell. Mitchell believes he has reached god status and sees humans as instruments and creatures to be used for his pleasure, comfort, and amusement. With the help of another god, Kirk survives his ordeal and conquers Mitchell.

In "The Enemy Within," Kirk, the mortal, has his good and evil parts separated. Apart neither Kirks are able to perform either morally or competently.

The dichotomy of the human spirit is exposed and analyzed revealing that mortal man must have within him the seeds of destructive and aggressive tendencies and the moral and ethical gatekeeper to keep it in check. Mortals are not like gods and therefore must behave in a manner acceptable to society.

In, "Dagger of the Mind," Kirk, still our mortal man, must withstand the evils of another mortal man, who aspires to be a god. Doctor Adams' thirst for power and control nearly drains Kirk's strength of will. In the end, Adams becomes a victim of his own folly of mind control, thus telling us that mortal man may not become gods through acts of deception and manipulation. We must attain godhood by other means.

TOS was born out of the Cold War era. World War II and the Korean War were still fresh in our minds and the Vietnam War was just getting into full swing. As a country, we were changing our morals and re-evaluating what it was to be an American. TOS, consensually conscious or unconscious, was telling us that mistrust, unregulated power, misguided control, and unbridled lust would, could, and should lead to our destruction.

Collectively, we, as a group of humans, sat in front of a television and watched a show that, like some other shows before it, tried to put into perspective the meaning of our morale values. We watched and absorbed the interplay between man and would-be gods, between good, evil, and a mixture of both; we sat, watched, and enjoyed this show. It exposed our soft underbelly and let us look into the Emperor's mirror where we became beholden to our spirits. We witnessed the nakedness of our souls and questioned who we were, are and shall be. This show became our Odyssey and our Troy and our Gomorrah. It reflected us. This show was known as Star Trek.

KAREN BECHARD
UN AGENT
I FEAR NO EVIL WHEN DUTY CALLS I AM A GLOBAL CITIZEN SOLDIER
BOOK TRAILER
ACTION ADVENTURE

Strange Star Likely Swarmed by Comets

A star called KIC 8462852 has been in the news recently for unexplained and bizarre behavior. NASA's Kepler mission had monitored the star for four years, observing two unusual incidents, in 2011 and 2013, when the star's light dimmed in dramatic, never-before-seen ways. Something had passed in front of the star and blocked its light, but what?

Scientists first reported the findings in September, suggesting a family of comets as the most likely explanation. Other cited causes included fragments of planets and asteroids.

A new study using data from NASA's Spitzer Space Telescope addresses the mystery, finding more evidence for the scenario involving a swarm of comets. The study, led by Massimo Marengo of Iowa State University, Ames, is accepted for publication in the Astrophysical Journal Letters.

One way to learn more about the star is to study it in infrared light. Kepler had observed it in visible light. If a planetary impact, or a collision amongst asteroids, were behind the mystery of KIC 8462852, then there should be an excess of infrared light around the star. Dusty, ground-up bits of rock would be at the right temperature to glow at infrared wavelengths.

At first, researchers tried to look for infrared light using NASA's Wide-Field Infrared Survey Explorer, or WISE, and found none. But those observations were taken in 2010, before the strange events seen by Kepler -- and before any collisions would have kicked up dust.

To search for infrared light that might have been generated after the oddball events, researchers turned to Spitzer, which, like WISE, also detects infrared light. Spitzer just happened to observe KIC 8462852 more recently in 2015.

"Spitzer has observed all of the hundreds of thousands of stars where Kepler hunted for planets, in the hope of finding infrared emission from circumstellar dust," said Michael Werner, the Spitzer project scientist at NASA's Jet Propulsion Laboratory in Pasadena, California, and the lead investigator of that particular Spitzer/Kepler observing program.

But, like WISE, Spitzer did not find any significant excess of infrared light from warm dust. That makes theories of rocky smashups very unlikely, and favors the idea that cold comets are responsible. It's possible that a family of comets is traveling on a very long, eccentric orbit around the star. At the head of the pack would be a very large comet, which would have blocked the star's light in 2011, as noted by Kepler. Later, in 2013, the rest of the comet family, a band of varied fragments lagging behind, would have passed in front of the star and again blocked its light.

By the time Spitzer observed the star in 2015, those comets would be farther away, having continued on their long journey around the star. They would not leave any infrared signatures that could be detected.

According to Marengo, more observations are needed to help settle the case of KIC 8462852.

"This is a very strange star," he said. "It reminds me of when we first discovered pulsars. They were emitting odd signals nobody had ever seen before, and the first one discovered was named LGM-1 after 'Little Green Men.'"

In the end, the LGM-1 signals turned out to be a natural phenomenon.

"We may not know yet what's going on around this star," Marengo observed. "But that's what makes it so interesting."

Ames manages the Kepler and K2 missions for NASA's Science Mission Directorate. JPL managed Kepler mission development. Ball Aerospace &

Technologies Corp. operates the flight system with support from the Laboratory for Atmospheric and Space Physics at the University of Colorado in Boulder.

JPL manages the Spitzer Space Telescope mission for NASA's Science Mission Directorate, Washington. Science operations are conducted at the Spitzer Science Center at the California Institute of Technology in Pasadena. Spacecraft operations are based at Lockheed Martin Space Systems Company, Littleton, Colorado. Data are archived at the Infrared Science Archive housed at the Infrared Processing and Analysis Center at Caltech.

Caltech manages JPL for NASA.

For more information about Kepler and Spitzer, respectively, visit:

http://www.nasa.gov/kepler

http://kepler.nasa.gov

http://www.nasa.gov/spitzer

http://www.spitzer.caltech.edu

Media Contact

Whitney Clavin
Jet Propulsion Laboratory, Pasadena, California
818-354-4673
whitney.clavin@jpl.nasa.gov

Michele Johnson
Ames Research Center, Moffett Field, Calif.
650-604-6982
michele.johnson@nasa.gov

2015-357

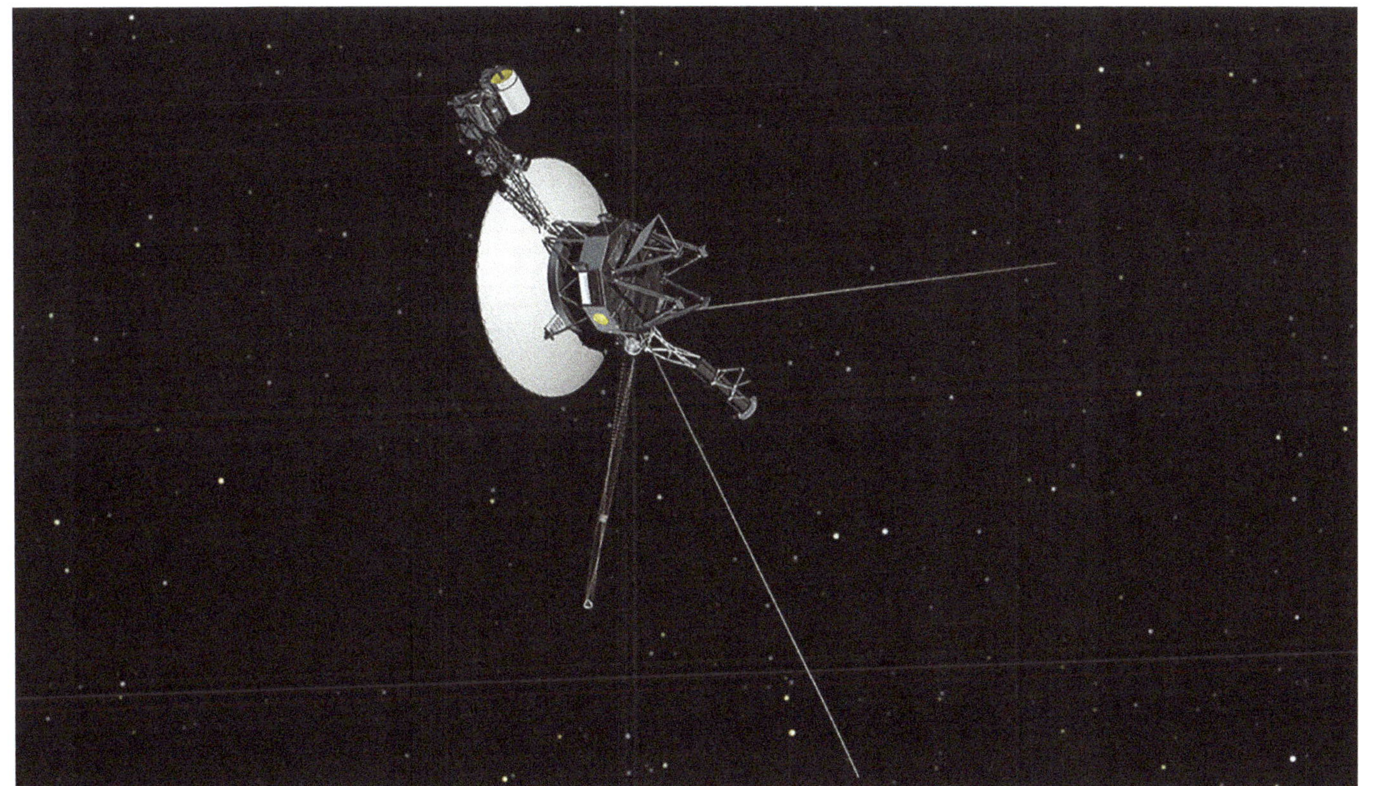

Voyager 1 Helps Solve Interstellar Medium Mystery

NASA's Voyager 1 spacecraft made history in 2012 by entering interstellar space, leaving the planets and the solar wind behind. But observations from the pioneering probe were puzzling with regard to the magnetic field around it, as they differed from what scientists derived from observations by other spacecraft.

A new study offers fresh insights into this mystery. Writing in the Astrophysical Journal Letters, Nathan Schwadron of the University of New Hampshire, Durham, and colleagues reanalyzed magnetic field data from Voyager 1 and found that the direction of the magnetic field has been slowly turning ever since the spacecraft crossed into interstellar space. They believe this is an effect of the nearby boundary of the solar wind, a stream of charged particles that comes from the sun.

"This study provides very strong evidence that Voyager 1 is in a region where the magnetic field is being deflected by the solar wind," said Schwadron, lead author of the study.

Researchers predict that in 10 years Voyager 1 will reach a more "pristine" region of the interstellar medium where the solar wind does not significantly influence the magnetic field.

Voyager 1's crossing into interstellar space meant it had left the heliosphere -- the bubble of solar wind surrounding our sun and the planets. Observations from Voyager's instruments found that the particle density was 40 times greater outside this boundary than inside, confirming that it had indeed left the heliosphere.

But so far, Voyager 1's observation of the direction of the local interstellar magnetic field is more than 40 degrees off from what other spacecraft have determined. The new study suggests this discrepancy exists because Voyager 1 is in a more distorted magnetic field just outside the heliopause, which is the boundary between the solar wind and the interstellar medium.

"If you think of the magnetic field as a rubber band stretched around a beach ball, that band is being deflected around the heliopause," Schwadron said.

In 2009, NASA's Interstellar Boundary Explorer (IBEX) discovered a "ribbon" of energetic neutral atoms that is thought to hold clues to the direction of the pristine interstellar magnetic field. The so-called "IBEX ribbon," which forms a circular arc in the sky, remains mysterious, but scientists believe it is produced by a flow of neutral hydrogen atoms from the solar wind that were re-ionized in nearby interstellar space and then picked up electrons to become neutral again.

The new study uses multiple data sets to confirm that the magnetic field direction at the center of the IBEX ribbon is the same direction as the magnetic field in the pristine interstellar medium. Observations from the NASA/ESA Ulysses and SOHO spacecraft also support the new findings.

"All of these different data sets that have been collected over the last 25 years have been pointing toward the same meeting point in the field," Schwadron said.

Over time, the study suggests, at increasing distances from the heliosphere, the magnetic field will be oriented more and more toward "true north," as defined by the IBEX ribbon. By 2025, if the field around Voyager 1 continues to steadily turn, Voyager 1 will observe the same magnetic field direction as IBEX. That would signal Voyager 1's arrival in a less distorted region of the interstellar medium.

"It's an interesting way to look at the data. It gives a prediction of how long we'll have to go before Voyager 1 is in the medium that's no longer strongly perturbed," said Ed Stone, Voyager project scientist, based at the California Institute of Technology in Pasadena, who was not involved in this study.

While Voyager 1 will continue delivering insights about interstellar space, its twin probe Voyager 2 is also expected to cross into the interstellar medium within the next few years. Voyager 2 will make additional observations of the magnetic field in interstellar space and help scientists refine their estimates.

Voyager 1 and Voyager 2 were launched 16 days apart in 1977. Both spacecraft flew by Jupiter and Saturn. Voyager 2 also flew by Uranus and Neptune. Voyager 2, launched before Voyager 1, is the longest continuously operated spacecraft. Voyager 1 is the most distant object touched by human hands.

JPL, a division of Caltech, built the twin Voyager spacecraft and operates them for the Heliophysics Division within NASA's Science Mission Directorate in Washington.

For more information about Voyager, visit:

http://voyager.jpl.nasa.gov

Media Contact

Elizabeth Landau
NASA's Jet Propulsion Laboratory, Pasadena, Calif.
818-354-6425
Elizabeth.Landau@jpl.nasa.gov

2015-334

Experience Curiosity Screen Capture

http://eyes.nasa.gov/curiosity/

A screen capture from NASA's new Experience Curiosity website shows the rover in the process of taking its own self-portrait. Users can view Mars through the eyes of the rover, using the window in the lower, right corner. The control panel at left helps users navigate the rover itself, and relive some of its actual expeditions on Mars.

Visit the website online at: http://eyes.nasa.gov/curiosity/ .

Image Credit: NASA/JPL-Caltech

This artist's concept depicts Kepler-186f, the first validated Earth-size planet to orbit a distant star in the habitable zone -- a range of distance from a star where liquid water might pool on the planet's surface. The discovery of Kepler-186f confirms that Earth-size planets exist in the habitable zones of other stars and signals a significant step closer to finding a world similar to Earth.

The size of Kepler-186f is known to be less than ten percent larger than Earth, but its mass, composition and density are not known. Previous research suggests that a planet the size of Kepler-186f is likely to be rocky. Prior to this discovery, the "record holder" for the most "Earth-like" planet went to Kepler-62f, which is 40 percent larger than the size of Earth and orbits in its star's habitable zone.

Kepler-186f orbits its star once every 130 days and receives one-third the energy that Earth does from the sun, placing it near the outer edge of the habitable zone. If you could stand on the surface of Kepler-186f, the brightness of its star at high noon would appear as bright as our sun is about an hour before sunset on Earth.

Kepler-186f resides in the Kepler-186 system about 500 light-years from Earth in the constellation Cygnus. The system is also home to four inner planets, seen lined up in orbit around a host star that is half the size and mass of the sun.

The artistic concept of Kepler-186f is the result of scientists and artists collaborating to imagine the appearance of these distant worlds.

NASA Ames manages Kepler's ground system development, mission operations and science data analysis. NASA's Jet Propulsion Laboratory in Pasadena, Calif., managed Kepler mission development. Ball Aerospace & Technologies Corp. in Boulder, Colo., developed the Kepler flight system and supports mission operations with JPL at the Laboratory for Atmospheric and Space Physics at the University of Colorado in Boulder. The Space Telescope Science Institute in Baltimore archives, hosts and distributes the Kepler science data. Kepler is NASA's 10th Discovery Mission and is funded by NASA's Science Mission Directorate at the agency's headquarters in Washington.

More information about the Kepler mission is at **http://www.nasa.gov/kepler**.

TACHYON NODE

Of Reunions
Kenneth A Strickland
Of Reunions
Kenneth A
Strickland
Available
April 2016
When a father makes a mistake, it is his to correct . . .
before his planet kills the son he doesn't know.
Published by Mythical Legends Publishing, LLC

Bibliography

Moshe Prigan

Moshe Prigan is a writer of short fiction and is currently writing a book. He lives in Haifa, Israel and he is a graduate of Haifa University in History and Political Sciences. His Hebrew stories have been published by Biglal Magazine and Stematsky's The Literary Greenhouse Anthology. His English fiction has been published in magazines as The Bear (Ireland), Tales from the Shadow Realm, Genesis Science Fiction, 34th Parallel, Witch Works, Fuck Fiction and A Quiet Courage. Another fiction is forthcoming in HOOT.

Patricia I Williams

Born in New Orleans, La. and lived in Alexandria until she was twelve, Patricia I. Williams fell in love with Southern California on arrival. She would not want to live anywhere else, at least for this lifetime. She loves knowing the ocean is just beyond the hill and that Disneyland is the happiest place on earth. She enjoys traveling through the Southwest. The history and legends fuel a lot of imaginative Wild West adventures. She loves Science Fiction, film and books. Believes horses, dogs and cats are ideal companions.

Kenneth A Strickland

Kenneth Strickland was born in 1958, a very good year because he showed up! He has a love for science fiction although he hasn't read everyone others say he should, he enjoys it greatly. He is a grad of Westchester High School in Los Angeles, enjoys history, auto racing and animation. (No, he doesn't know the words to Let it Go...) Loves art, and loves taking the bus to the end of the line to see where it goes. He loves cooking, cars and music. He has studied comedy and film and animation and is working with a professional friend to produce a web series. He has worked in retail, and as a security guard (most boring!). Generally speaking, I like you when I meet you. Enjoys being a nerd. My first book was a joy to write, and I hope you enjoy it.

Jarita Holbrook

Jarita Holbrook is Associate Professor of Physics at the University of the Western Cape. She writes American multicultural science fiction and her fantasy short stories can be found in Genesis: An Anthology of Black Science Fiction Volume II, edited by Jarvis Sheffield; and Griots : sisters of the spear, edited by Milton J Davis and Charles R Saunders. She considers her science fiction 'American' because she tries to capture those particular race relations in her writings. She is in the process of completing her forthcoming four volume science fiction series Astronaut Tribe. Dr. Holbrook holds degrees in physics, astronomy, and astrophysics from Caltech (BS), San Diego State University (MS), and UC Santa Cruz (PhD). She is an expert on African Indigenous Astronomy and she studies the practices of inclusion and exclusion among astrophysicists.

Bibliography

Brandon Hill

I am a native of Louisiana and current resident of Lafayette. An avid and frequent reader of science fiction and fantasy, I began writing in the eleventh grade. I am a graduate of McNeese State University in Lake Charles.

"I am a 'classic nerd' and hopeless romantic who loves sci-fi and fantasy, and am a prolific writer who has had dreams of authorship since childhood. I sketch perhaps even more prolifically than I write, and have drawings of just about every character my warped imagination has come up with. I hope to continue sharing these ideas, characters, and stories with others for years to come."

Tonya Moore

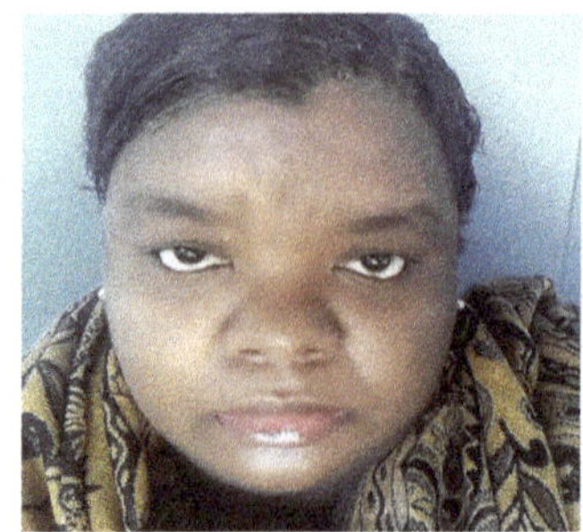

Tonya R. Moore writes science fiction, fantasy and horror short stories and novellas. She is the author of the ongoing web serial godpunk/urban fantasy, Firecracker, at JukePopSerials.com.

Tonya grew up reading books by the likes of phenomenal authors such as Isaac Asimov, Ray Bradbury, Larry Niven and Anne McCaffrey. Their works portrayed space-faring humans and unbelievable creatures having fantastic adventures in distant future and far-flung regions of the universe. She fell in love with the remarkable characters and worlds they envisioned. Those stories fueled her desire to write.

Tonya hails from the island of Jamaica, but currently calls Bradenton, Florida home.

Devon Nicholson

My Name is Devon Nicholson. I am 24 years old and I am currently living in Savannah , GA. I spend my days lost in a sea of code and data hoping to save enough money to pursue my true passion, game design. If I'm not working, playing music, or fumbling through adulthood I often escape to the worlds of fantasy and fiction. Writing is freeing and I hope to one day be known for my ability to tell a good story.

J Carrell Jones

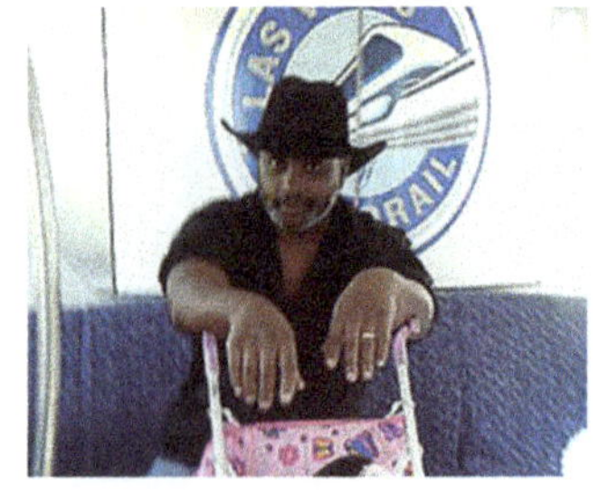

Born and raised in Southern California, J Carrell Jones, an Army Veteran, has worked in the Customer Support field for nearly 30 years. His interests are as vast as his imagination - 3D Content creating to writing to graphic design to voice overs. Currently, he lives in Inglewood, California with his wife, a beautiful daughter, a female cat named Perilous, a dozen fish, and two guinea pigs. The oldest is Hop and the younger one is named Guinea.